THE BOOK OF MARK

THE STORY OF JESUS

A STUDYGUIDE IN SIMPLIFIED ENGLISH

SHARI PLUEDDEMANN MAXWELL

Harold Shaw Publishers, Wheaton, Illinois
Neighborhood Bible Studies Inc., Dobbs Ferry, New York

Material in this studyguide has been adapted from *Mark* © 1963 by Marilyn Kunz and Catherine Schell, published by Neighborhood Bible Studies. This edition in simplified English is published by special arrangement between Neighborhood Bible Studies and Harold Shaw Publishers.

Grateful acknowledgment is made to Christian Literature International for permission to use the entire text of the book of Mark, taken from the *Holy Bible, NEW LIFE Version,* © 1969, 1976, 1978, 1983, 1986 by Christian Literature International, P.O. Box 777, Canby, Oregon 97013. (*NOTE:* Wherever an * is seen in the Scripture text, the words that follow are not in all the early writings of the New Testament. If part of a verse is missing in some of the early writings, it is marked with an (*).)

ISBN 0-87788-518-4

Cover photo © 1999 by Image Technologies

03   02   01   00   99

10   9   8   7   6   5   4   3   2   1

CONTENTS

This book will help you learn for yourself what the Bible says. The book uses three kinds of questions:

1. Questions to help you learn what the Bible story says.

2. Questions to help you understand what the Bible story means.

3. Questions to help you see how the Bible story may make a difference in your life.

The following pictures show the types of questions:

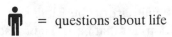

= questions about life

= questions from the Bible

= questions that bring the Bible into your life

It is good to have a different person ask the questions each week.

Each Bible study takes about an hour. Think about how much time you want to add for praying and talking with people in your group.

Ideas for a good Bible Study

1. Each person needs a study book.

2. Use a dictionary for words we do not use every day.

3. Try not to talk about things that are not in the Bible story.

4. The Bible is the authority in the group, not the people.

5. Listen to other people in the group to help you think about what the story means.

6. Practice what the Bible says.

7. Read the story and think about the questions before you come to the Bible study.

8. Begin and end on time.

Ideas for the person asking the questions

1. Read the Bible story several times. Ask God to help you understand it. Think about the answers to the questions.

2. In each study, you read a small part of the Bible story. The group answers the questions for that part. Then read the next part of the Bible story. If people in your group feel comfortable, ask different ones to read the Bible out loud. Or you may divide into groups of two. Take turns reading. Be careful not to ask people to read out loud if they do not want to.

3. Read the question. Wait for an answer. Be careful not to answer the question out loud yourself.

4. If some people talk too much say, "When I read the next question, let's hear from someone who hasn't said anything yet today."

5. Ask one person to ask the questions for the next study.

Would you like to hear from a person who knew Jesus Christ? Read the Book of Mark. It is the first story we have of the life of Jesus. It was written about A.D. 65. Mark wrote the story of Christ's life as Peter (who was a follower of Jesus) told it to him.

Who was Mark? The Bible tells us interesting things about the life of Mark. The house of Mark's mother, Mary, was the main meeting place for the Christians in Jerusalem. As a young man, Mark went on the first trip to tell the Jews and Gentiles about Jesus with his cousin Barnabas and the follower Paul. He left them before the end of the trip. On the next trip Paul did not want to take Mark with them. Barnabas took Mark with him. Paul went with Silas. Later, Mark became a strong Christian. Twelve years later he helped Paul who was in prison in Rome. Paul wrote about Mark in his letter to Timothy.

In this book Mark answers the question "Who is Jesus Christ?" As we study this story of Jesus' life, we will see who he is. Someone said that Mark's Gospel could be called the most important book in the world.

Mark 1:1-28

John The Baptist Makes The Way Ready For The Coming Of Jesus

1 [1] The Good News of Jesus Christ, the Son of God, [2] begins with the words of the early preachers: "Listen! I will send My helper to carry the news ahead of you. He will make the way ready. [3] His voice calls out in the desert, 'Make the way ready for the Lord. Make the road straight for Him!' " (Isaiah 40:3) [4] John the Baptist preached in the desert. He preached that people should be baptized because they were sorry for their sins and had turned from them. And they would be forgiven. [5] People from over all the country of Judea and from Jerusalem came to him. They told of their sins and were baptized by John in the Jordan River.

[6] John wore clothes made of hair from camels. He had a leather belt around him. His food was locusts and wild honey. [7] He preached, saying, "One is coming after me Who is greater than I. I am not good enough to get down and help Him take off His shoes. [8] I have baptized you with water. But He will baptize you with the Holy Spirit."

The Baptism Of Jesus

[9] Jesus came to the Jordan River from the town of Nazareth in the country of Galilee. He was baptized by John. [10] As soon as Jesus came up out of the water, He saw heaven open up. The Holy Spirit came down on Him like a dove. [11] A voice came from heaven and said, "You are My much-loved Son. I am very happy with You."

Jesus Was Tempted

[12] At once the Holy Spirit sent Jesus to a desert. [13] He was tempted by Satan for forty days there. He was with wild animals but angels took care of Him.

Jesus Preaches In Galilee

[14] After John the Baptist was put in prison, Jesus came to the country of Galilee. He preached the Good News of God. [15] He said, "The time has come. The holy nation of God is near. Be sorry for your sins, turn from them, and believe the Good News."

Jesus Calls Simon And Andrew

[16] Jesus was walking by the Sea of Galilee. He saw Simon and his brother Andrew putting a net into the sea. They were fishermen. [17] Jesus said to them, "Follow Me. I will make you fish for men!" [18] At once they left their nets and followed Him.

Jesus Calls James And John

[19] Jesus went on a little farther. He saw James and his brother John who were sons of Zebedee. They were in a boat mending their nets. [20] Jesus called them and they left their father Zebedee. He was in the boat with men who were working for him.

Jesus Heals A Man With A Demon

[21] Jesus and His followers went to the city of Capernaum on the Day of Rest. They went to the Jewish place of worship where Jesus taught the people. [22] The people were surprised and wondered about His teaching. He taught them as One Who had the right and the power to teach and not as the teachers of the Law.

[23] There was a man in the Jewish place of worship who had a demon. The demon cried out, [24] "What do You want of us, Jesus of Nazareth? Have You come to destroy us? I know Who You are. You are the Holy One of God." [25] Jesus spoke sharp words to the demon and said, "Do not talk! Come out of the man!" [26] The demon threw the man down and gave a loud cry. Then he came out of him. [27] The people were all surprised and wondered. They asked each other, "What is this? Is this a new teaching? He speaks with power even to the demons and they obey Him!" [28] At once the news about Jesus went through all the country around Galilee.

Jesus Begins His Work

Mark 1:1-28

Who is Jesus? Is he a great teacher? Is he a prophet? Is he the Son of God? This is the most important question anyone can ask. Mark wrote this book to answer this important question.

Read Mark 1:1-8

1. What is the best news you have ever heard?

    Who gave you the news?

2. John the Baptist brings news that Jewish people waited hundreds of years to hear. What will John the Baptist do (verses 2, 3)?

3. What does John the Baptist tell the people to do?

    What do the people do when they hear John preach (verse 5)?

4. What news does John give the people about Christ who will come soon (verses 7, 8)?

5. How do people hear about the Good News of Jesus today?

Read Mark 1:9-15

6. Find Nazareth, Jerusalem, and the Jordan River on the map on page 154 in this study guide. When does Jesus come from Nazareth to the Jordan River (verses 4, 9)?

7. What unusual things happen at Jesus' baptism (verses 10, 11)?

8. What is temptation?

9. Why does Jesus go into the desert (verse 12)?

   Who tempts Jesus when he is in the desert (verses 12, 13)?

   Who takes care of Jesus?

10. Find Galilee on your map on page 154. What good news does Jesus preach in Galilee (verses 14, 15)?

11. What do you need to do if you obey Jesus' teaching?

Read Mark 1:16-20

12. What kind of followers do leaders choose today?

13. What kind of people does Jesus ask to follow him (verses 16, 19, 20)?

   Why do you think Jesus asks these people to follow him instead of other well-known religious leaders?

14. What does Jesus say to these men (verse 17)?

    How do they answer Jesus (verses 18, 20)?

 15. How does Jesus ask people to follow him today?

    What do other people think when someone decides to follow Jesus?

Read Mark 1:21-28

 16. Who is someone you know that has a lot of power?

 17. Where is Jesus teaching (verse 21)?

18. How is Jesus' teaching different from others (verse 22)?

19. Describe what happens while Jesus is teaching (verses 23-27).

    Who does the demon say Jesus is (verse 24)?

    Who are the demons afraid of?

20. Where does Jesus' power come from (verses 11, 14)?

 21. If you know that Jesus has complete power, how can that make a difference in your life?

Summary

1. What do you learn about Jesus?

2. How does Mark begin to show that Jesus is the Son of God?

Prayer

Dear Jesus,
Thank you for teaching me more about who you are. I see in you great power that helps people. Amen.

Mark 1:29-45

Peter's Mother-in-Law Healed

1 ²⁹ Jesus and His followers came out of the Jewish place of worship. Then they went to the house of Simon and Andrew. James and John went with them. ³⁰ They told Jesus about Simon's mother-in-law who was in bed, very sick.³¹ He went and took her by the hand and raised her up. At once her sickness was gone. She got up and cared for them.

Jesus Heals In Galilee

³² In the evening as the sun went down, the people took all who were sick to Jesus. They took those who had demons to Him. ³³ All the town gathered at the door. ³⁴ Jesus healed those who were sick of many kinds of diseases. He put out many demons. Jesus would not allow the demons to speak because they knew Who He was.

Jesus Keeps On Preaching In Galilee

³⁵ In the morning before the sun was up, Jesus went to a place where He could be alone. He prayed there. ³⁶ Simon and the others looked for Jesus. ³⁷ They found Him and said, "All the people are looking for You." ³⁸ Jesus said to the followers, "Let us go to the towns near here so I can preach there also. That is why I came." ³⁹ He went through Galilee. He preached in their places of worship and put out demons.

Jesus Heals A Man With A Bad Skin Disease

⁴⁰ A man came to Jesus with a bad skin disease. This man got down on his knees and begged Jesus, saying, "If You want to, You can heal me." ⁴¹ Jesus put His hand on him

with loving-pity. He said, "I want to. Be healed." [42] At once the disease was gone and the man was healed. [43] Jesus spoke strong words to the man before He sent him away. [44] He said to him, "Tell no one about this. Go and let the religious leader of the Jews see you. Give the gifts Moses has told you to give when a man is healed of a disease. Let the leaders know you have been healed." [45] But the man went out and talked about it everywhere. After this Jesus could not go to any town if people knew He was there. He had to stay in the desert. People came to Him from everywhere.

Jesus Has Power to Heal

Mark 1:29-45

J esus shows his love for people by healing many kinds of diseases. Where does Jesus get the power to heal? Look for the answer to this question as you study.

Read Mark 1:29-34

 1. What do people today do when someone is very sick?

2. What do Jesus' followers do when Peter's mother-in-law is very sick (verse 30)?

Note: The Jews could not work or travel on the Sabbath until after it ended at sundown.

3. How does Jesus show his power in this story (verses 31 and 34) ?

4. Why do you think Jesus would not want the demons to say who he is?

Read Mark 1:35-39

 5. Why do people pray?

 6. Look at verses 21-34. What are all the things Jesus does in one day?

7. Where does Jesus go very early the next morning (verse 35)?

8. Why do you think Jesus prays?

9. Why does Jesus not go back and heal more people (verse 38)?

10. What does Jesus do (verse 39)?

 11. How does prayer help us make decisions about what is most important in our lives?

Read Mark 1:40-45

 12. List diseases that people are afraid to be close to.

 13. What does the man with the bad skin disease want Jesus to do (verse 40)?

14. How does Jesus answer him (verses 41, 42)?

15. Why is it important that Jesus touches this man?

16. Why does Jesus tell the man healed of the bad skin disease not to tell anyone how he got well (verses 43, 44)?

17. What happens because the man does not obey Jesus?

18. How can you show love to those you are afraid to touch?

Summary

1. What do you think about Jesus from what you have learned so far?

2. How does Mark begin to show that Jesus is the Son of God?

Prayer

Dear Jesus,
Thank you for teaching me more about who you are. I see great power in you when you heal. Thank you for showing me that prayer is important. Amen.

Mark 2:1–3:6

Jesus Heals A Man Who Was Let Down
Through The Roof Of A House

2 [1] After some days Jesus went back to the city of Capernaum. Then news got around that He was home. [2]Soon many people gathered there. There was no more room, not even at the door. He spoke the Word of God to them. [3]Four men came to Jesus carrying a man who could not move his body. [4] These men could not get near Jesus because of so many people. They made a hole in the roof of the house over where Jesus stood. Then they let down the bed with the sick man on it. [5] When Jesus saw their faith, He said to the sick man, "Son, your sins are forgiven." [6]Some teachers of the Law were sitting there. They thought to themselves, [7] "Why does this Man talk like this? He is speaking as if He is God! Who can forgive sins? Only One can forgive sins and that is God!" [8] At once Jesus knew the teachers of the Law were thinking this. He said to them, "Why do you think this in your hearts? [9] Which is easier to say to the sick man, ' Your sins are forgiven,' or to say, 'Get up, take your bed, and start to walk?' [10] I am doing this so you may know the Son of Man has power on earth to forgive sins." He said to the sick man who could not move his body, [11] "I say to you, 'Get up. Take your bed and go to your home.' " [12] At once the sick man got up and took his bed and went away. Everybody saw him. They were all surprised and wondered about it. They thanked God, saying, "We have never seen anything like this!"

Jesus Calls Matthew

[13] Jesus walked along the seashore again. Many people came together and He taught them. [14] He walked farther and saw

Levi (Matthew) the son of Alphaeus. Levi was sitting at his work gathering taxes. Jesus said to him, "Follow Me." Levi got up and followed Him.

Jesus Eats With Tax-gatherers And Sinners

[15] Jesus ate in Levi's house. Many men who gather taxes and others who were sinners came and sat down with Jesus and His followers. There were many following Him. [16] The teachers of the Law and the proud religious law-keepers saw Jesus eat with men who gather taxes and others who were sinners. They said to His followers, "Why does He eat and drink with men who gather taxes and with sinners?" [17] Jesus heard it and said to them, "People who are well do not need a doctor. Only those who are sick need a doctor. I have not come to call those who are right with God. I have come to call those who are sinners."

Jesus Teaches About Going Without Food So You Can Pray Better

[18] The followers of John and the proud religious law-keepers were not eating food so they could pray better. Some people came to Jesus and said, "Why do the followers of John and the proud religious law-keepers go without food so they can pray better, but Your followers do not?" [19] Jesus said to them, "Can the friends at a wedding go without food when the man just married is with them? As long as they have him with them, they will not go without food. [20] The days will come when the man just married will be taken from them. Then they will not eat food so they can pray better. [21] No man sews a piece of new cloth on an old coat. If it comes off, it will make the hole bigger. [22] No man puts new wine into old skin bags. The skin would break and the wine would run out. The bags would be no good. New wine must be put into new skin bags."

Jesus Teaches About The Day Of Rest

[23] At that time Jesus walked through the grain-fields on the Day of Rest. As they went, His followers began to take some of the grain. [24] The proud religious law-keepers said

to Jesus, "See! Why are they doing what the Law says should not be done on the Day of Rest?" [25] He said to them, "Have you not read what David did when he and his men were hungry? [26] He went into the house of God when Abiathar was head religious leader of the Jews. He ate the special bread used in the religious worship. The Law says only the Jewish religious leaders may eat that. David gave some to those who were with him also." [27] Jesus said to them, "The Day of Rest was made for the good of man. Man was not made for the Day of Rest. [28] The Son of Man is Lord of the Day of Rest also."

Jesus Heals On The Day Of Rest

3 [1] Jesus went into the Jewish place of worship again. A man was there with a dried-up hand. [2] The proud religious law-keepers watched Jesus to see if He would heal the man on the Day of Rest. They wanted to have something to say against Jesus. [3] Jesus said to the man with the dried-up hand, "Stand up." [4] Then Jesus said to the proud religious law-keepers, "Does the Law say to do good on the Day of Rest or to do bad, to save life or to kill?" But they said nothing. [5] Jesus looked around at them with anger. He was sad because of their hard hearts. Then He said to the man, "Put out your hand." He put it out and his hand was healed. It was as good as the other. [6] The proud religious law-keepers went out and made plans with the followers of King Herod how they might kill Jesus.

Opposite Ideas

Mark 2:1–3:6

Mark shows us who Jesus is through his teaching. His ideas are new and different. As you study today, think about these two questions: What do the people think when they hear Jesus preach and see his miracles? What do you think about Jesus?

Read Mark 2:1-12

1. What are the biggest needs people have today?
   security, peace, love, comfort, food, medscine

2. Jesus did many things when he was in Capernaum the first time. He taught in the place of worship, put out demons, and healed the sick. Describe what happens while Jesus teaches in Capernaum again (verses 3, 4). *A guad is brot to Jesus through a roof crowds incl Pharisees*

3. What do you think the man's friends want Jesus to do? *Heal him*   *believed   would*

   How is that different from what Jesus says in verse 5? *He forgives sins rather than heals Heals souls rather than body.*

4. What do the teachers of the Law think about Jesus' words (verses 6, 7)? *He thinks He's God!*
   Blasphemy

5. What does Jesus want to show the teachers when he heals the man who can not walk (verse 10)?
   That He has the power to heal.

6. How does the man show that he believes in Jesus (verse 12)? *Did as told*

7. What do the people think about the way Jesus heals this man (verse 12)? *Surprise, Amazed, Wondrous*

8. How can Jesus help you with your biggest needs?
   Belief = healing - prayer amid   Peace

9. How can you help your friends with their biggest needs? *Be available   Pray for them   Cook*

Read Mark 2:13-17

10. In the place where you live, what kinds of people are difficult to like or respect? *Street people, psych, F word users*
    Cheaters, liars

11. What kind of man does Jesus ask to follow him (verse 14)? *Tax collector*

    How does Levi introduce Jesus to his friends?
    Over a meal
    Note: Jews hated the tax collectors because they worked for the Romans who ruled the land. They made extra money for what they took in from the people.

12. What do the teachers of the Law think of Jesus' actions (verse 16)? *Strange   Wrong!*

Note: Teachers of the Law were a group of religious Jews who obeyed the Law of Moses and many rules added to it. They are also known as Pharisees.

13. What does Jesus say to these proud teachers about himself, and what he has come to do (verse 17)?

He has come to show sinners the way

Read Mark 2:18-22

14. In what ways do people today follow rules of religion without understanding why they do it?

15. When people fast, they do not eat food. Some people ask Jesus why his disciples do not fast. How does Jesus' story about the wedding answer their question (verses 19, 20)?

16. In this story what is like the old cloth and old wine skin bags (verses 18, 21, 22)? *Practise of fasting = New lessons Jesus teaches adherence to law*

    In this story what is like the new cloth and new wine skin bags (verses 18, 21, 22)? *Fun, compassion*

17. Jesus is teaching new things that people have different ideas about. What do you think about Jesus' teachings in verses 10, 17, 18-20?

Presbyterians could learn from them. Learn new ways

Read Mark 2:23-28

18. What do the proud religious law-keepers complain about (verses 23, 24)? *Breaking the law*

19. What does Jesus say about the Day of Rest (verse 27)? *It was made for man. Man needs to rest*

Note: Sabbath - The seventh day of the Jewish week was a day of rest from any work.

20. What does Jesus say about himself (verse 28)?

He is Lord on the Day of Rest, also.

Read Mark 3:1-6

21. Why do some of the people watch Jesus on the Day of Rest in the place of worship (verse 2)?

To see if he would heal the man

What question does Jesus ask the people who watch him? *Does the law say to do good, or bad?*

Note: In Jesus' time, over a thousand rules made the Sabbath a heavy burden instead of a day of rest.

22. What different feelings does Jesus have (verse 5)?

anger   sadnesse

Why? *because of their lack of compassion*

23. What do the religious leaders do after Jesus heals this man (verse 6)? *plot his death ō Herod*

Note: Usually Pharisees did not agree with the followers of King Herod, a Jewish political group that supported him.

24. What different ideas do people today have about Jesus, and why?

Summary

1. What ideas do the religious leaders have opposite to the ideas of Jesus, and why?

2. In each story what does Jesus teach us about himself? *He is loving, compassionate, caring inclusive, power.*

3. If you believe and do what Jesus teaches, how will your life be different?

Prayer

Dear Jesus,
Thank you for loving every person, even the ones who are sick and full of sin. Thank you for loving me. Amen.

Read Mark 3:7-35

Jesus Heals By The Sea-shore

3 ⁷ Jesus went with His followers to the sea. Many people followed Him from the countries of Galilee and Judea. ⁸ They followed from Jerusalem and from the country of Idumea. They came from the other side of the Jordan River and from the cities of Tyre and Sidon. Many people heard all that Jesus was doing and came to Him. ⁹ He told His followers to have a small boat ready for Him because so many people might push Him down. ¹⁰ He had healed so many that the sick people were pushing in on Him. They were trying to put their hands on Him. ¹¹ When demons saw Him, they got down at His feet and cried out, "You are the Son of God!" ¹² He spoke strong words that the demons should tell no one Who He was.

Jesus Calls His Twelve Followers

¹³ He went up on a mountain and called those He wanted. They followed Him. ¹⁴ He picked out twelve followers to be with Him so He might send them out to preach. ¹⁵ They would have the right and the power to heal diseases and to put out demons. ¹⁶ Jesus gave Simon another name, Peter. ¹⁷ James and John were brothers. They were the sons of Zebedee. He named them Boanerges, which means, The Sons of Thunder. ¹⁸ The others were Andrew, Philip, Bartholomew, Matthew, Thomas, James the son of Alphaeus, Thaddaeus, Simon the Canaanite, ¹⁹ and Judas Iscariot. Judas was the one who handed Jesus over to be killed.

The Family Of Jesus Holds Him Back

[20] When Jesus came into a house, many people gathered around Him again. Jesus and His followers could not even eat. [21] When His family heard of it, they went to take Him. They said, "He must be crazy."

A Nation That Cannot Stand

[22] Teachers of the Law came down from Jerusalem. They said, "Jesus has Satan in Him. This Man puts out demons by the king of demons." [23] Jesus called them to Him and spoke to them in picture-stories. He said, "How can the devil put out the devil? [24] A nation cannot last if it is divided against itself. [25] A family cannot last if it is divided against itself. [26] If the devil fights against himself and is divided, he cannot last. He will come to an end. [27] No man can go into a strong man's house and take away his things, unless he ties up the strong man first. Only then can he take things from his house. [28] For sure, I tell you, all sins will be forgiven people, and bad things they speak against God. [29] But if anyone speaks bad things against the Holy Spirit, he will never be forgiven. He is guilty of a sin that lasts forever." [30] Jesus told them this because they said, "He has a demon."

The New Kind Of Family

[31] Then His mother and brothers came and stood outside. They sent for Jesus. [32] Many people were sitting around Him. They said, "See! Your mother and brothers are outside looking for You." [33] He said to them, "Who is My mother or My brothers?" [34] He turned to those sitting around Him and said, "See! My mother and My brothers! [35] Whoever does what My Father wants is My brother and My sister and My mother."

People Ask Questions about Jesus' Power

Read Mark 3:7-35

Many people know who Jesus is now. Some people like him and some don't. What do the crowds, teachers of the Law, and Jesus' family think about him? Read Mark's story to find out.

Read Mark 3:7-12

1. What are some reasons people gather in large crowds today? *Hear, See, Learn*

2. Look on the map on page 154. How far do people come to see Jesus (verses 7, 8)? *80-90 miles to Sea of Galilee*

   How has Jesus' ministry grown since Mark 1:28? *Galilee*

   Why do so many people come to Jesus (verse 8)?
   They heard what he was doing. Healing

3. What do the people with demons in them do when they see Jesus (verse 11)? *Kneel + name him "Son of God".*

4. Why doesn't Jesus want the demons to let other people know who he is (verse 12)?
   The time wasn't right.

5. In this story people walk a long way to come to Jesus. How do people hear about Jesus today?
Radio, TV, church, preachers

Read Mark 3:13-19

6. What does Jesus want the twelve followers to do (verses 14, 15)? *preach, heal, cast out demons*

Note: Another name for the twelve followers of Jesus is Apostles, who are special messengers.

7. What is important about the order of these three things?

8. To which three followers does Jesus give another name (verse 16, 17)? *Simon, James, John*
   "Peter"   "Sons of Thunder"

9. Why do we usually give nicknames?
   endearment, familiarity

   What are some other facts that you learn about the twelve Jesus chose (verses 16-19)?
   J+J = bros. + sons of Zebedee   Son of Alphaeus = James
   Simon = Canaanite Zealot Judas betrayed Jesus

10. What kind of followers does Jesus need today?
    everyone

Read Mark 3:20-30

11. What do people you know think about Jesus?
    depends

12. What does Jesus' family do when they hear about what is going on (verses 20-22)? *Go to take him home*

13. What do the teachers of the Law think about Jesus (verse 22)? *Called him "Satan"*

    How does Jesus answer them (verses 23-27)?
    A house against itself cannot stand   A. Lincoln

14. Where does Jesus get his power (1:10, 11)?
    God via Holy Spirit

15. What bad things do the teachers of the Law say against the Holy Spirit (verses 22, 30)?
    He's a demon

16. What danger are these people in (verses 28-30)?
    Eternal damnation

Read Mark 3:31-35

17. Describe what happens in verses 31-35.
    Jesus' family call him. He responds, "Everyone is my family."

18. Who does Jesus say are his brother, sister, and mother? *Everyone*

19. What is the most important thing in following Jesus (verse 35)? *Do what God wants.*

Summary

1. In chapters 1 and 2, Jesus does powerful things. What are good and bad responses from the people in chapter 3? *Belief*   *Disbelief*

2. The people around Jesus think many different things about him. What do people today think about those who choose to follow Jesus?
   Admire   *Disgust*

Prayer

Dear Jesus,
Many people have questions about the power that you have in healing, teaching, and telling demons to leave. Help me to understand who you are and what it means to follow you. Amen.

Mark 4:1-34

The Picture-story Of The Man Who Planted Seed

4 ¹ Jesus began to teach by the seashore again. Many people gathered around Him. There were so many He had to get into a boat and sit down. The people were on the shore. ²He taught them many things by using picture-stories. As He taught, He said, ³ "Listen! A man went out to plant seed. ⁴ As he planted the seed, some fell by the side of the road. Birds came and ate them. ⁵ Some seed fell among rocks. It came up at once because there was so little ground. ⁶ But it dried up when the sun was high in the sky because it had no root. ⁷ Some seed fell among thorns. The thorns grew and did not give the seed room to grow. This seed gave no grain. ⁸ Some seed fell on good ground. It came up and grew and gave much grain. Some gave thirty times as much grain. Some gave sixty times as much grain. Some gave one hundred times as much grain." ⁹ He said to them, "You have ears, then listen!" ¹⁰ Those who were with Jesus and the twelve followers came to Him when He was alone. They asked about the picture-story. ¹¹ He said to them, "You were given the secrets about the holy nation of God. Everything is told in picture-stories to those who are outside the holy nation of God. ¹² They see, but do not know what it means. They hear, but do not understand. If they did, they might turn to God and have their sins forgiven."

Jesus Tells About The Man Who Planted The Seed

¹³ Jesus said to them, "Do you not understand this picture-story? Then how will you understand any of the picture-stories? ¹⁴ What the man plants is the Word of God. ¹⁵ Those by the side of the road are the ones who hear the Word. As soon as they hear it, the devil comes and takes away the

Word that is planted in their hearts. [16] The seed that fell among rocks is like people who receive the Word with joy when they hear it. [17] Their roots are not deep so they live only a short time. When sorrow and trouble come because of the Word, they give up and fall away. [18] The seed that was planted among thorns is like some people who listen to the Word. [19] But the cares of this life let thorns come up. A love for riches and always wanting other things let thorns grow. These things do not give the Word room to grow so it does not give grain. [20] The seed that fell on good ground is like people who hear the Word and understand it. They give much grain. Some give thirty times as much grain. Some give sixty times as much grain. Some give one hundred times as much grain."

The Picture-story Of The Lamp

[21] He said to them, "Is a lamp to be put under a pail or under a bed? Should it not be put on a lamp-stand? [22] Everything that is hidden will be brought into the light. Everything that is a secret will be made known. [23] You have ears, then listen!" [24] Jesus said to them, "Be careful what you listen to. The same amount you give will be given to you, and even more. [25] He who has, to him will be given. To him who does not have, even the little he has will be taken from him."

The Picture-story Of The Grain

[26] He said, "The holy nation of God is like a man who plants seed in the ground. [27] He goes to sleep every night and gets up every day. The seed grows, but he does not know how. [28] The earth gives fruit by itself. The leaf comes first and then the young grain can be seen. And last, the grain is ready to gather. [29] As soon as the grain is ready, he cuts it. The time of gathering the grain has come."

The Picture-story Of The Mustard Seed

[30] Jesus said, "In what way can we show what the holy nation of God is like? Or what picture-story can we use to help you understand? [31] It is like a grain of mustard seed that is planted in the ground. It is the smallest of all seeds. [32] After

it is put in the ground, it grows and becomes the largest of the spices. It puts out long branches so birds of the sky can live in it." [33] As they were able to understand, He spoke the Word to them by using many picture-stories. [34] Jesus helped His followers understand everything when He was alone with them.

Picture Stories

Mark 4:1-34

J esus uses stories to teach people truth. When you read these stories, look to see how people learn about Jesus and what Jesus' plan is for the world.

Read Mark 4:1-9

1. How do stories help people learn? *visualization*

2. How does Jesus begin and end his picture-story in verses 3 and 9? *" Listen "*

   Why is this important? *must pay attention to understand*

3. Describe the four kinds of ground that the seeds fall on (verses 4, 5, 7, 8). *Road, rock, thorns, fertile*

Read Mark 4:10-20

4. Who asks Jesus to explain his picture-story (verse 10)? *those present + Hi's 12,*

5. Why do some people understand his picture-stories and some do not (verse 11)? *His followers + not*

6. What difference does it make in people's lives when they understand Jesus' picture-stories (verse 12)?

   Sins would be forgiven.

7. What does Jesus compare the seeds to in this story (verse 14)? *the Word of God*

8. Describe what happens to the four kinds of people who hear God's message (verses 15-20).

   How are they the same?

   How are they different?

9. How do the things in verse 19 keep God's Word from changing people's lives today?

   How does the Word of God change your life?

Read Mark 4:21-25

10. What happens if you don't practice what you learn from a teacher?

11. Jesus uses picture-stories to teach people. What does he say about his teaching (verses 21-23)?

    It should be shared

12. Look at verses 9 and 23. Why is it important to pay attention to God's Word (verses 8, 20)? *Profit*

13. What happens if you listen and practice Jesus' teaching (verse 24, 25)? *you will profit*

14. What happens if you do not think carefully about Jesus' teaching (verse 25)?

    you will lose

Read Mark 4:26-34

15. Describe something that starts small and then grows into something very big. *gossip, Equinox dinner, life, faith, addictions*

16. The holy nation of God (the kingdom of God) is where God rules and shows his power. Look at the story in verses 26-29. Describe how the rule of God begins and grows in our hearts.

17. Look at verses 30-33. Describe how the holy nation of God begins and grows in the world.

18. In what ways do you see the holy nation of God growing in yourself and in countries around the world? *missionaries*

Summary

1. What do you learn about the holy nation of God (the kingdom of God) from these picture-stories?

2. Why do you think Jesus says it is important to hear, listen, and obey the Word of God?

3. What keeps you from understanding Jesus' teaching?

   What helps you hear, listen, and follow Jesus' teaching?

Prayer

Dear Jesus,
I pray that the Word of God will grow from something
small to something very big in my life. Amen.

Mark 4:35–5:43

The Wind And Waves Obey Jesus

4 [35] It was evening of that same day. Jesus said to them, "Let us go over to the other side." [36] After sending the people away, they took Jesus with them in a boat. It was the same boat He used when He taught them. Other little boats went along with them. [37] A bad wind storm came up. The waves were coming over the side of the boat. It was filling up with water. [38] Jesus was in the back part of the boat sleeping on a pillow. They woke Him up, crying out, "Teacher, do You not care that we are about to die?" [39] He got up and spoke sharp words to the wind. He said to the sea, "Be quiet! Be still." At once the wind stopped blowing. There were no more waves. [40] He said to His followers, "Why are you so full of fear? Do you not have faith?" [41]They were very much afraid and said to each other, "Who is this? Even the wind and waves obey Him!"

Demons Ask Jesus To Let Them Live In Pigs

5 [1] Jesus and His followers came to the other side of the sea to the country of the Gerasenes. [2] He got out of the boat. At once a man came to Him from among the graves. This man had a demon. [3] He lived among the graves. No man could tie him, even with chains. [4] Many times he had been tied with chains on his feet. He had broken the chains as well as the irons from his hands and legs. No man was strong enough to keep him tied. [5] Night and day he was among the graves and in the mountains. He would cry out and cut himself with stones.

[6] When the man with the demon saw Jesus a long way off, he ran and worshiped Him. [7] The man spoke with a loud voice and said, "What do You want with me, Jesus, Son of the Most High God? I ask You, in the name of God, do not hurt me!" [8] At the same time, Jesus was saying, "Come out of the man, you demon!" [9] Jesus asked the demon, "What is your name?" He said, "My name is Many, for there are many of us." [10] The demons asked Jesus not to send them out of the country. [11] There were many pigs feeding on the mountain side. [12] The demons asked Him saying, "Send us to the pigs that we may go into them." [13] Then Jesus let them do what they wanted to do. So they went into the pigs. The pigs ran fast down the side of the mountain and into the sea and died. There were about 2,000. [14] The men who cared for the pigs ran fast to the town and out to the country telling what had been done. People came to see what had happened. [15] They came to Jesus and saw the man who had had the demons. He was sitting with clothes on and in his right mind. The men were afraid. [16] Those who had seen it told what had happened to the man who had had the demons. They told what had happened to the pigs. [17] Then they asked Jesus to leave their country.

[18] Jesus got in the boat. The man who had the demons asked to go with Him. [19] Jesus would not let him go but said to him, "Go home to your own people. Tell them what great things the Lord has done for you. Tell them how He had pity on you." [20] The man went his way and told everyone in the land of Decapolis what great things Jesus had done for him. All the people were surprised and wondered.

Two Were Healed Through Faith

[21] Then Jesus went by boat over to the other side of the sea. Many people gathered around Him. He stayed by the seashore. [22] Jairus was one of the leaders of the Jewish place of worship. As Jairus came to Jesus, he got down at His feet. [23] He cried out to Jesus and said, "My little daughter is almost dead. Come and put your hand on her that she may be healed and live." [24] Jesus went with him. Many people followed and pushed around Jesus.

[25] A woman had been sick for twelve years with a flow of blood. [26] She had suffered much because of having many

doctors. She had spent all the money she had. She had received no help, but became worse. [27] She heard about Jesus and went among the people who were following Him. She touched His coat. [28] For she said to herself, "If I can only touch His coat, I will be healed." [29] At once the flow of blood stopped. She felt in her body that she was healed of her sickness. [30] At the same time Jesus knew that power had gone from Him. He turned and said to the people following Him, "Who touched My coat?" [31] His followers said to Him, "You see the many people pushing on every side. Why do You ask, 'Who touched My coat?' " [32] He looked around to see who had done it. [33] The woman was filled with fear when she knew what had happened to her. She came and got down before Jesus and told Him the truth. [34] He said to her, "Daughter, your faith has healed you. Go in peace and be free from your sickness." [35] While Jesus spoke, men came from the house of the leader of the place of worship. They said, "Your daughter is dead. Why trouble the Teacher anymore?" [36] Jesus heard this. He said to the leader of the Jewish place of worship, "Do not be afraid, just believe." [37] He allowed no one to go with Him but Peter and James and John, the brother of James. [38] They came to the house where the leader of the place of worship lived. Jesus found many people making much noise and crying. [39] He went in and asked them, "Why is there so much noise and crying? The girl is not dead. She is sleeping."

[40] They laughed at Jesus. But He sent them all out of the room. Then He took the girl's father and mother and those who were with Him. They went into the room where the girl was. [41] He took the girl by the hand and said, "Little girl, I say to you, get up!" [42] At once the girl got up and walked. She was twelve years old. They were very much surprised and wondered about it. [43] He spoke sharp words to them that they should not tell anyone. He told them to give her something to eat.

Jesus Helps People with Difficult Problems

Mark 4:35–5:43

J esus' followers learn about him as he helps people with difficult problems. Read to see how Jesus' power helps the people in these stories.

Read Mark 4:35-41

1. How does Mark describe this storm (verse 37)?

2. After teaching all day, Jesus is sound asleep in the back of the boat. Why do his followers wake him up (verse 38)?

3. How does Jesus solve this problem (verse 39)?

4. Why do you think Jesus asks his followers the questions in verse 40?

5. How do Jesus' followers feel in verse 38 and in verses 40 and 41?

   How is this miracle different from the other miracles before this?

6. Think about problems in your life. How does this story help you?

Read Mark 5:1-20

7. What do verses 2-5 tell us about this man?

8. What do you learn about demons (verses 6-13)?

9. What three things are different about the man after Jesus sends the demons out of him (verses 3-5, 15)?

    How do you think the people in the town and country feel about Jesus (verses 13-17)?

Note: This story happens on the east shore of Lake Galilee where people were not Jews. This may be why Jesus does some things differently here.

10. How do you think the man who had the demons feels about Jesus (verses 18-20)?

11. What do people today think about Jesus' power?

Read Mark 5:21-24

12. Who is Jairus and what does he need (verses 22, 23)?

    Describe his faith (verse 23).

Read Mark 5:25-34

13. What do you learn about the woman in verses 25 and 26?

14. How do people who are sick for a long time feel?

15. What does this woman believe about Jesus (verses 27, 28)?

16. What is different about the ways this woman and Jairus ask for healing (verses 23 and 28)?

Note: Under Jewish law this woman's sickness made her unclean, and anyone who touched her would be thought unclean.

17. How does talking to Jesus help her (verses 33, 34)?

18. What kinds of sicknesses do people have today that are embarrassing to tell others about?

Read Mark 5:35-43

19. How do you think Jairus feels in verses 23-35?

20. What does Jesus say to Jairus (verse 36)?

21. Describe what Jesus does in verses 37-43.

22. Why does Jesus tell the parents to give the girl something to eat (verse 43)?

23. In what parts of your life do you need Jesus to help you?

Summary

1. What are the four things that Jesus shows his power over in this study?

2. What do the people do in each of these stories when Jesus shows his power?

3. What does Jesus want you to do today when you see Jesus' power?

Prayer

Dear Jesus,
You help people by showing your power in very difficult situations. Help me to trust your power in my difficult problems. Amen.

Mark 6

Jesus Visits His Own Town, Nazareth

6 ¹ Jesus went from the house of Jairus and came to His home town. His followers came after Him. ²On the Day of Rest He began to teach in the Jewish place of worship. Many people heard Him. They were surprised and wondered, saying, "Where did this Man get all this? What wisdom is this that has been given to Him? How can He do these powerful works with His hands? ³ Is He not a Man Who makes things from wood? Is He not the Son of Mary and the brother of James and Joses and Judas and Simon? Do not His sisters live here with us?" The people were ashamed of Him and turned away from Him. ⁴Jesus said to them, "One who speaks for God is respected everywhere but in his own country and among his own family and in his own house."

⁵ So Jesus could do no powerful works there. But He did put His hands on a few sick people and healed them. ⁶He wondered because they had no faith. But He went around to the towns and taught as He went.

Jesus Calls Twelve Followers And Sends Them Out

⁷Jesus called the twelve followers to Him and began to send them out two by two. He gave them power over demons. ⁸He told them to take nothing along with them but a walking stick. They were not to take a bag or food or money in their belts. ⁹They were to wear shoes. They were not to take two coats.

¹⁰ He said to them, "Whatever house you go into, stay there until you leave that town. ¹¹ Whoever does not take you in or listen to you, when you leave there, shake the dust off your feet. By doing that, you will speak against them.

For sure, I tell you, it will be easier for the cities of Sodom and Gomorrah on the day men stand before God and are judged than for that city."

[12] Then they left. They preached that men should be sorry for their sins and turn from them. [13] They put out many demons. They poured oil on many people that were sick and healed them.

John The Baptist Is Put In Prison

[14] King Herod heard about Jesus because everyone was talking about Him. Some people said, "John the Baptist has been raised from the dead. That is why he is doing such powerful works." [15] Other people said, "He is Elijah." Others said, "He is one who speaks for God like one of the early preachers." [16] When Herod heard this, he said, "It is John the Baptist, whose head I cut off. He has been raised from the dead." [17] For Herod had sent men to take John and put him into prison. He did this because of his wife, Herodias. She had been the wife of his brother Philip. [18]John the Baptist had said to Herod, "It is wrong for you to have your brother's wife." [19] Herodias became angry with him. She wanted to have John the Baptist killed but she could not. [20] Herod was afraid of John. He knew he was a good man and right with God, and he kept John from being hurt or killed. He liked to listen to John preach. But when he did, he became troubled.

John The Baptist Is Killed

[21] Then Herodias found a way to have John killed. Herod gave a big supper on his birthday. He asked the leaders of the country and army captains and the leaders of Galilee to come. [22] The daughter of Herodias came in and danced before them. This made Herod and his friends happy. The king said to the girl, "Ask me for whatever you want and I will give it to you." [23] Then he made a promise to her, "Whatever you ask for, I will give it to you. I will give you even half of my nation." [24] She went to her mother and asked, "What should I ask for?" The mother answered, "I want the head of John the Baptist." [25] At once the girl went

to Herod. She said, "I want you to give me the head of John the Baptist on a plate now."

[26] Herod was very sorry. He had to do it because of his promise and because of those who ate with him. [27] At once he sent one of his soldiers and told him to bring the head of John the Baptist. The soldier went to the prison and cut off John's head. [28] He took John's head in on a plate and gave it to the girl. The girl gave it to her mother. [29] John's followers heard this. They went and took his body and buried it.

The Feeding Of The Five Thousand

[30] The followers of Jesus came back to Him. They told Jesus all they had done and taught. [31] He said to them, "Come away from the people. Be by yourselves and rest." There were many people coming and going. They had had no time even to eat. [32] They went by themselves in a boat to a desert. [33] Many people saw them leave and knew who they were. People ran fast from all the cities and got there first. [34] When Jesus got out of the boat He saw many people gathered together. He had loving-pity for them. They were like sheep without a shepherd. He began to teach them many things.

[35] The day was almost gone. The followers of Jesus came to Him. They said, "This is a desert. It is getting late. [36] Tell the people to go to the towns and villages and buy food for themselves." [37] He said to them, "Give them something to eat." They said to Him, "Are we to go and buy many loaves of bread and give it to them?" [38] He said to them, "How many loaves of bread do you have here? Go and see." When they knew, they said, "Five loaves of bread and two fish." [39] Then He told them to have all the people sit down together in groups on the green grass. [40] They sat down in groups of fifty people and in groups of one hundred people. [41] Jesus took the five loaves of bread and two fish. He looked up to heaven and gave thanks. He broke the loaves in pieces and gave them to the followers to set before the people. He divided the two fish among them all. [42] They all ate and were filled. [43] After that the followers picked up twelve baskets full of pieces of bread and fish. [44] About five thousand men ate the bread.

Jesus Walks On The Water

[45] At once Jesus had His followers get into the boat and go ahead of Him to the other side to the town of Bethsaida. He sent the people away. [46] When they were all gone, He went up to the mountain to pray. [47] It was evening. The boat was half-way across the sea. Jesus was alone on the land. [48] He saw His followers were in trouble. The wind was against them. They were working very hard rowing the boat. About three o'clock in the morning Jesus came to them walking on the sea. He would have gone past them. [49] When the followers saw Him walking on the water, they thought it was a spirit and cried out with fear. [50] For they all saw Him and were afraid. At once Jesus talked to them. He said, "Take hope. It is I, do not be afraid." [51] He came over to them and got into the boat. The wind stopped. They were very much surprised and wondered about it. [52] They had not learned what they should have learned from the loaves because their hearts were hard.

People Are Healed At Gennesaret

[53] Then they crossed the sea and came to the land of Gennesaret and went to shore. [54] When Jesus got out of the boat, the people knew Him at once. [55] They ran through all the country bringing people who were sick on their beds to Jesus. [56] Wherever He went, they would lay the sick people in the streets in the center of town where people gather. They begged Him that they might touch the bottom of His coat. Everyone who did was healed. This happened in the towns and in the cities and in the country where He went.

What Is It Like to Follow Jesus?

Mark 6

This chapter shows us what it is like to be a follower of Jesus. In our lives today we can see the same good things and the same problems of these first followers of Jesus. Many have questions about who Jesus is. Jesus' family, Herod, and Jesus' followers all have questions about him.

Read Mark 6:1-6

1. What do people in your home town think when someone leaves and then comes back with more power or money?

2. What do the people in Jesus' home town think about him (verses 2, 3)?

3. What stops Jesus from working there (verses 4-6)?

4. What might happen in your home town if you tell people you are a follower of Jesus?

Read Mark 6:7-13

5. What power and what special instructions does Jesus give the twelve followers (verses 7-11)?

   Why do you think Jesus gives them these instructions?

6. What is the same in the followers' message (6:12), John's message (1:4), and Jesus' message (1:15)?

7. What do the twelve followers do?

   How will their work help to spread the message of Jesus?

Read Mark 6:14-29

8. Who do King Herod and others think Jesus is (verses 14, 15)?

9. Why did Herod refuse to accept John's message (verses 17, 18)?

   How did Herod feel about John (verse 20)?

10. Why do people today fail to do what they know is right?

Read Mark 6:30-44

11. Why does Jesus decide to take his followers away (verses 12, 13, 30, 31)?

   What happens as soon as they leave (verses 33, 34)?

12. What is the difference in the way his followers and Jesus think about the problem (verses 34-37)?

13. How do you think the followers feel in verse 37 and in verse 43?

14. What can you learn in this story of five loaves of bread and two fish feeding five thousand people?

Read Mark 6:45-52

15. What kinds of things make you feel afraid or frustrated?

How do you act in these times?

16. John 6:14, 15 says that this crowd wants to make Jesus king when they see him feed five thousand people. Why does Jesus tell the followers to go ahead of him in the boat (verse 45)?

Why do you think Jesus needs to pray at this time (verse 46)?

17. What problems do the followers have in the boat (verses 47, 48)?

How does Jesus help them (verses 49-51)?

18. What difficult things have the twelve followers had to do in one long day (verses 32-52)?

19. Why do the followers have hard hearts (verse 52)?

20. What do you think Jesus is trying to show his followers?

What don't they understand (verse 52)?

 21. How does this story help you know what to do when you feel frustrated or afraid?

22. What happens when Jesus and the twelve stop in the land of Gennesaret?

Why does Jesus continue to be so popular?

Summary

1. Three groups of people in this chapter do not understand Jesus. What keeps the people in Jesus' hometown, Herod, and the followers of Jesus all from understanding him?

2. What makes it difficult for you to follow Jesus?

3. How can you learn to have Jesus' love for people?

Prayer

Dear Jesus,
Thank you for feeding so many people who ran to hear you, with your message and then with bread and fish. Thank you for healing the sick brought by their friends. Help me to understand who you are and then how to follow you. Amen.

Mark 7

Jesus Speaks Sharp Words To The Leaders

7 [1] The proud religious law-keepers and some of the teachers of the Law had come from Jerusalem. They gathered around Jesus. [2] They had seen some of His followers eat bread without washing their hands. [3] The proud religious law-keepers and all the Jews never eat until they wash their hands. They keep the teaching that was given to them by their early fathers. [4] When they come from the stores, they never eat until they wash. There are many other teachings they keep. Some are the washing of cups and pots and pans in a special way.

[5] Then the proud religious law-keepers and the teachers of the Law asked Jesus, "Why do Your followers not obey the teaching given to them by their early fathers? They eat bread without washing their hands." [6] He said to them, "Isaiah told about you who pretend to be someone you are not. Isaiah wrote, 'These people honor Me with their lips, but their hearts are far from Me. Their worship of Me is worth nothing. They teach what men say must be done.' You put away the Laws of God and obey the laws made by men."

[9] Jesus said to them, "You put away the Laws of God but keep your own teaching. [10] Moses said, 'Respect your father and mother.' 'He who curses his father and mother will be put to death!' [11] But you say that it is right if a man does not help his father and mother because he says he has given to God what he could have given to them. [12] You are not making him do anything for his father and mother. [13] You are putting away the Word of God to keep your own teaching. You are doing many other things like this."

[14] Jesus called the people to Him again. He said, "Listen to Me, all of you, and understand this. [15] It is not what goes

into a man's mouth from the outside that makes his mind and heart sinful. It is what comes out from the inside that makes him sinful. [16] You have ears, then listen!"

[17] He went into the house away from all the people. His followers began to ask about the picture-story. [18] He said to them, "Do you not understand yet? Do you not understand that whatever goes into a man cannot make him sinful? [19] It does not go into his heart, but into his stomach and then on out of his body." In this way, He was saying that all food is clean. [20] He said, "Whatever comes out of a man is what makes the man sinful. [21] From the inside, out of the heart of men come bad thoughts, sex sins of a married person, sex sins of a person not married, killing other people, stealing, wanting something that belongs to someone else, doing wrong, lying, having a desire for sex sins, having a mind that is always looking for sin, speaking against God, thinking you are better than you are and doing foolish things. [23] All these bad things come from the inside and make the man sinful."

Jesus Puts A Demon Out Of A Girl

[24] Jesus went from their towns and cities to the cities of Tyre and Sidon. He went into a house and wanted to stay there without people knowing where He was. But He could not hide Himself. [25] A woman who had a daughter with a demon heard of Him. She came and got down at His feet. [26] The woman was not a Jew. She was from the country of Syrophenicia. She asked Jesus if He would put the demon out of her daughter. [27] Jesus said to her, "Let the children have what they want first. It is wrong to take children's food and throw it to the dogs." [28] She said to Him, "Yes, Lord, but even the dogs eat the pieces that fall from the children's table." [29] He said to her, "Because of what you have said, go your way. The demon is gone out of your daughter." [30] So she went to her house and found the demon was gone and her daughter was lying on the bed.

Jesus Heals The Man Who Could Not Hear Or Speak Well

[31] Then Jesus left the cities of Tyre and Sidon. He came back to the Sea of Galilee by way of the land of Decapolis. [32] They took a man to Him who could not hear or speak well. They asked Jesus to put His hand on him. [33] Jesus took him away from the other people. He put His fingers into the man's ears. He spit and put His finger on the man's tongue. [34] Then Jesus looked up to heaven and breathed deep within. He said to the man, "Be opened!" [35] At once his ears were opened. His tongue was made loose and he spoke as other people. [36] Then Jesus told them they should tell no one. The more He told them this, the more they told what He had done. [37] They were very much surprised and wondered about it. They said, "He has done all things well. He makes those who could not hear so they can hear. He makes those who could not speak so they can speak."

What Makes People Clean?

Mark 7

S ome people think it is important to follow many rules to please God. The religious leaders in Jesus' time were like that. They had more than six hundred rules for everyday life! Jesus spoke to them strongly because he could see inside their hearts and he knew they were sinful. Their rules covered up their real problem.

Read Mark 7:1-8

 1. What were some of the rules in your family when you were growing up?

2. Why do the proud law-keepers and some teachers of the Law complain to Jesus about his followers (verses 2, 5)?

Note: The teachers say people's hands are not clean unless they are washed in a special way.

3. How does Jesus answer them (verses 6-16)?

What does he call them (verse 6)?

4. What does Jesus say about their rules (verses 7, 8)?

5. Why do we often obey rules people make instead of God's teaching?

Read Mark 7:9-13

6. What is Moses' teaching about how we should act toward our parents (verse 10)?

7. What action toward parents do some teachers of the law say is right (verses 11, 12)?

8. Do you think there are people today who try to change God's laws?

   Why?

Read Mark 7:14-23

9. How does Jesus show that his teaching is very important (verse 14)?

10. What does not make a person sinful (verses 15, 18)?

11. What does make a person sinful (verses 15)?

12. Look at verses 21-23. What is first on the list?

    What other things come after? How well does this list fit our world today?

13. Instead of washing the outside, what kind of cure do people need for their sinfulness?

Read Mark 7:24-30

Find the cities of Tyre and Sidon on the map, and find
the Sea of Galilee and the land of Decapolis on the map
(page 154).

14. Tell about a time when you felt like a stranger.

15. The woman who comes to Jesus is not a Jew. Why
    does she come to Jesus (verse 25)?

    How does Jesus answer her?

16. What can you learn from this woman's example
    about coming to Jesus?

Read Mark 7:31-37

17. Tell about a time when you needed other people to
    help you.

18. Who asks Jesus to heal the man who could not hear
    or speak (verse 32)?

19. What things does Jesus do when he heals the man
    (verses 33-35)?

    How would these help the deaf man know what Jesus
    plans to do?

20. What do the people do and say when Jesus heals the
    man (verses 36, 37)?

21. How could you help a friend who needs Jesus?

Summary

1. What is the most important need people have?

2. How does Jesus want us to come to him?

Prayer

Dear Jesus,
I understand more clearly now that you are the only one who can change my heart. I ask you to make me completely clean. Amen.

Mark 8:1–9:1

The Feeding Of The Four Thousand

8 [1] In those days many people were gathered together. They had nothing to eat. Jesus called His followers to Him and said, [2] "I pity these people because they have been with Me three days and have nothing to eat. [3] If I send them home without food, they may be too weak as they go. Many of them have come a long way."

[4] His followers said to Him, "Where can anyone get enough bread for them here in this desert?" [5] He asked them, "How many loaves of bread do you have?" They said, "Seven." [6] Then He told the people to sit down on the ground. Jesus took the seven loaves of bread and gave thanks to God. He broke the loaves and gave them to His followers to give to the people. The followers gave the bread to them. [7] They had a few small fish also. He gave thanks to God and told the followers to give the fish to them. [8] They all ate and were filled. They picked up seven baskets full of pieces of bread and fish after the people were finished eating. [9] About four thousand ate. Then Jesus sent the people away.

The Proud Religious Law-keepers Ask For Something Special To See

[10] At once Jesus got in a boat with His followers and came to the country of Dalmanutha. [11] The proud religious law-keepers came and began to ask Him for something special to see from heaven. They wanted to trap Jesus. [12] He breathed deep within and said, "Why do the people of this day look for something special to see? For sure, I tell you, the people of this day will have nothing special to see from heaven." [13] Then He left them. He got in the boat and went to the other side of the sea.

Jesus Shows That The Teaching Of The Proud Religious Law-keepers Is Wrong

[14] The followers had forgotten to take bread, only one loaf was in the boat. [15] He said to them, "Look out! Have nothing to do with the yeast of the proud religious law-keepers and of Herod." [16] They talked about it among themselves. They said, "He said this because we forgot to bring bread." [17] Jesus knew what they were thinking. He said to them, "Why are you talking among yourselves about forgetting to bring bread? Do you not understand? Is it not plain to you? Are your hearts still hard? [18] You have eyes, do you not see? You have ears, do you not hear? Do you not remember? [19] When I divided the five loaves of bread among the five thousand, how many baskets full of pieces did you pick up?" They said, "Twelve." [20] "When I divided the seven loaves of bread among the four thousand, how many baskets full of pieces did you pick up?" They said, "Seven." [21] Then He asked, "Why do you not understand yet?"

Jesus Heals A Blind Man

[22] Then they came to the town of Bethsaida. Some people brought a blind man to Jesus. They asked if He would touch him. [23] He took the blind man by the hand out of town. Then He spit on the eyes of the blind man and put His hands on him. He asked, "Do you see anything?" [24] The blind man looked up and said, "I see some men. They look like trees, walking." [25] Jesus put His hands on the man's eyes again and told him to look up. Then he was healed and saw everything well. [26] Jesus sent him to his home and said, "Do not go into the town, *or tell it to anyone there."

Peter Says Jesus Is The Christ

[27] Jesus and His followers went from there to the towns of Caesarea Philippi. As they went, He asked His followers, "Who do people say that I am?" [28] They answered, "Some say John the Baptist and some say Elijah and others say oneof the early preachers." [29] He said to them, "But who do

you say that I am?" Peter said, "You are the Christ." [30] He told them with strong words that they should tell no one about Him.

Jesus Tells Of His Death For The First Time

[31] He began to teach them that the Son of Man must suffer many things. He told them that the leaders and the religious leaders of the Jews and the teachers of the Law would have nothing to do with Him. He told them He would be killed and three days later He would be raised from the dead.

[32] He had said this in plain words. Peter took Him away from the others and began to speak sharp words to Him. [33] Jesus turned around. He looked at His followers and spoke sharp words to Peter. He said, "Get behind Me, Satan! Your thoughts are not thoughts from God but from men."

Giving Up Self And One's Own Desires

[34] Jesus called the people and His followers to Him. He said to them, "If anyone wants to be My follower, he must give up himself and his own desires. He must take up his cross and follow Me. [35] If anyone wants to keep his own life safe, he will lose it. If anyone gives up his life because of Me and because of the Good News, he will save it. [36] For what does a man have if he gets all the world and loses his own soul? [37] What can a man give to buy back his soul? [38] Whoever is ashamed of Me and My words among the sinful people of this day, the Son of Man will be ashamed of him when He comes in the shining-greatness of His Father and His holy angels."

A Look At What Jesus Will Be Like

9 [1] Jesus said to them, "For sure I tell you, some standing here will not die until they see the holy nation of God come with power!"

What Does It Mean to Follow Jesus?

Mark 8:1–9:1

Mark teaches us why some choose to follow Christ and why others do not. What makes these people different? What do Jesus' followers need to do? Study this chapter to answer these questions.

Read Mark 8:1-10

1. Which lessons in life do you have to learn more than once?

2. What is different in this story from the story in 6:30-44?

   What do the followers of Jesus do in both stories?

3. How does Jesus feel about the people in both stories (6:34; 8:2-3)?

4. Jesus gives the people food and teaches them many things. How can you show others you care for both their physical and spiritual needs?

Read Mark 8:11-21

5. When do you question if Jesus will be able to help you even though he has helped you in the past?

6. Why do the proud religious law-keepers ask Jesus to do some miracle sign from heaven (verse 11)?

    Why doesn't Jesus do what they ask (verse 12)?

7. What is Jesus saying about the proud religious law-keepers (7:1-23) and about Herod (6:14-29) when he talks about the yeast?

    What do Jesus' followers think he is talking about (verse 16)?

8. What is Jesus telling his followers by the questions he asks in verses 17-21?

9. What is your answer if Jesus asks you some of these same questions?

    Is your heart still hard?

    Do you remember what Jesus teaches?

    Do you understand who Jesus is?

Read Mark 8:22-26

10. Who brings the blind man to Jesus (verse 22)?

11. Why do you think Jesus takes the blind man out of town?

---

12. Describe the way Jesus heals the blind man?

Read Mark 8:27-33

 13. Who do people today think Jesus is?

14. On the map on page 154, find the place where Jesus takes his followers. Why do you think Jesus goes this far north?

15. What is the difference in the two questions that Jesus asks his followers (verses 27, 29)?

    How do the followers answer the first question (verse 28)?

    How does Peter answer Jesus' second question (verse 29)?

16. After the followers believe that Jesus is the Christ (verse 29), what four things does Jesus begin to teach them (verse 31)?

17. When Peter hears these things, what does he do and say (verse 32)?

    Why?

    How do Jesus' words show that this is a time of temptation for him (verse 33)?

Note: The Jews at that time thought if the Messiah (the Christ) came he would free Israel from Rome's rule and become their king. But Jesus tells his followers he is going to die!

Read Mark 8:34–9:1

18. What does Jesus say people must do if they want to follow Him (verse 34)?

19. What are the two choices that are open to every person (verse 35)?

20. If people want to keep their life in this world by living to make themselves happy, what is the most they can do (verse 36)?

    What will happen to them in the end (verse 36)?

21. What does Jesus promise those who let go of their life to follow him (verse 35)?

22. Why do you think some people are ashamed of Jesus and his teaching?

    What will happen to these people in the future (verse 38)?

Summary

1. Who is Jesus? This is the most important question in the book of Mark. Find some of the answers Mark gives us:

   Mark   1:11
          1:24
          3:11
          4:41
          6:3
          6:14
          6:15
          8:29

2. Who do you think Jesus is?

   Why?

3. What do you need to do after you believe Jesus is the Christ?

Prayer

Dear Jesus,
Thank you for teaching me about who you are. Help me to make the right decisions about following you. Amen.

To be ready for the next study, please look at the instructions for the review of Mark 1–8 in Discussion 10.

Review of Mark 1–8

R ead chapters 1–8. Find what these chapters tell us about Jesus. Find what Jesus says, what he does, and what others say about him.

Each person in the group should choose one question to study. Be ready to tell your answers for that question to the group in this review meeting.

1. What does Jesus teach in these chapters about:

    -who he is?

    -why he came to earth?

    -his future?

2. What does Jesus teach about:

    -the holy nation of God (the kingdom of God)?

    -the Day of Rest?

    -what separates people from God?

    -what it means to be Jesus' follower?

3. What emotions does Jesus show towards individuals and groups?

    What kind of person does Jesus show he is by the things he does?

    How do Jesus' teachings show us what kind of person he is?

4. Describe Jesus' twelve followers.

    What do they see?

    What do they learn?

    How does their faith grow?

5. What do people think and do when they hear about Jesus?

    Who are the people who like Jesus?

    Who are the people who don't like Jesus?

    Why do these people have different ideas about Jesus?

6. From what you see in the first eight chapters of Mark, who do you think Jesus is?

    Where does he get his power?

Mark 9

A Look At What Jesus Will Be Like

9 [1] Jesus said to them, "For sure I tell you, some standing here will not die until they see the holy nation of God come with power!"

[2] Six days later Jesus took Peter and James and John with Him. He led them up to a high mountain by themselves. Jesus was changed as they looked at Him. [3] His clothes did shine. They were as white as snow. No one on earth could clean them so white. [4] Moses and Elijah were seen talking to Jesus.

[5] Peter said to Jesus, "Teacher, it is good for us to be here. Let us make three tents to worship in. One will be for You and one for Moses and one for Elijah." [6] Peter did not know what to say. They were very much afraid.

[7] A cloud came over them and a voice from the cloud said, "This is My much-loved Son. Listen to Him." [8] At once they looked around but saw no one there but Jesus.

[9] They came down from the mountain. Then Jesus said with strong words that they should tell no one what they had seen. They should wait until the Son of Man had risen from the dead. [10] So they kept those words to themselves, talking to each other about what He meant by being raised from the dead.

[11] They asked Jesus, "Why do the teachers of the Law say that Elijah must come first?" [12] He said to them, "For sure, Elijah will come first and get things ready. Is it not written that the Son of Man must suffer many things and that men will have nothing to do with Him? [13] But I say to you, Elijah has already come. They did to him whatever they wanted to do. It is written that they would."

A Boy With A Demon Is Healed

[14] When Jesus came back to His followers, He saw many people standing around them. The teachers of the Law were arguing with them. [15] The people saw Jesus and were surprised and ran to say hello to Him. [16] Jesus asked the teachers of the Law, "What are you arguing about with them?" [17] One of the people said, "Teacher, I brought my son to You. He has a demon in him and cannot talk. [18]Wherever the demon takes him, it throws him down. Spit runs from his mouth. He grinds his teeth. He is getting weaker. I asked Your followers to put the demon out but they could not."

[19] He said, "You people of this day have no faith. How long must I be with you? How long must I put up with you? Bring the boy to Me." [20] They brought the boy to Jesus. The demon saw Jesus and at once held the boy in his power. The boy fell to the ground with spit running from his mouth. [21] Jesus asked the boy's father, "How long has he been like this?" The father said, "From the time he was a child. [22]Many times it throws him into the fire and into the water to kill him. If You can do anything to help us, take pity on us!" [23] Jesus said to him, "Why do you ask Me that? The one who has faith can do all things." [24] At once the father cried out. He said with tears in his eyes, "Lord, I have faith. Help my weak faith to be stronger!" [25] Jesus saw that many people were gathering together in a hurry. He spoke sharp words to the demon. He said, "Demon! You who cannot speak or hear, I say to you, come out of him! Do not ever go into him again." [26] The demon gave a cry. It threw the boy down and came out of him. The boy was so much like a dead man that people said, "He is dead!" [27] But Jesus took him by the hand and helped him and he stood up.

[28] When Jesus went into the house, His followers asked Him when He was alone, "Why could we not put out the demon?" [29] He said to them, "The only way this kind of demon is put out is by prayer and by going without food so you can pray better."

Jesus Tells Of His Death The Second Time

[30] From there Jesus and His followers went through the country of Galilee. He did not want anyone to know where He was. [31] He taught His followers, saying, "The Son of Man will be handed over to men. They will kill Him. Three days after He is killed, He will be raised from the dead." [32] They did not understand what He said and were afraid to ask Him.

Jesus Teaches About The Faith Of A Child

[33] They came to the city of Capernaum and were in the house. Jesus asked His followers, "What were you arguing about along the road?" [34] They did not answer. They had been arguing along the road about who was the greatest. [35] Jesus sat down and called the followers to Him. He said, "If anyone wants to be first, he must be last of all. He will be the one to care for all."

[36] Jesus took a child and stood it among them. Then He took the child up in His arms and said to the followers, [37] "Whoever receives one of these little children in My name receives Me. Whoever will receive Me, receives not Me, but Him Who sent Me."

Jesus Speaks Sharp Words Against The Followers

[38] John said to Him, "Teacher, we saw someone putting out demons in Your name. We told him to stop because he was not following us." [39] Jesus said, "Do not stop him. No one who does a powerful work in My name can say anything bad about Me soon after. [40] The person who is not against us is for us. [41] For sure, I tell you, whoever gives you a cup of water to drink in My name because you belong to Christ will not lose his pay from God. [42] Whoever is the reason for one of these little ones who believes in Me to sin, it would be better for him to have a large stone put around his neck and to be thrown into the sea. [43] If your hand is the reason you fall into sin, cut it off. It is better to go into life without a hand, than to have two hands and go into the fire of hell that cannot be put out. [44] *There is where their worm never dies and the fire cannot be put out. [45] If your foot is the reason

you fall into sin, cut it off. It is better to go into life with only one foot, than to have two feet and go into the fire of hell that cannot be put out. [46] *There is where their worm never dies and the fire cannot be put out. [47] If your eye is the reason you fall into sin, take it out. It is better to go into the holy nation of God with only one eye, than to have two eyes and be thrown into the fire of hell. [48] There is where their worm never dies and the fire is never put out. [49] Everyone will be made cleaner and stronger with fire. [50]Salt is good. But if salt loses its taste, how can it be made to taste like salt again? Have salt in yourselves and be at peace with each other."

Belief and Unbelief

Mark 9

J esus' followers are still learning new things about him. Their faith is weak, but Jesus continues to show his power. Jesus knows his death is near. He wants to teach his friends the most important things about life. He and his followers begin the journey south to Jerusalem where he will die.

Read Mark 9:1-13

 1. Think about a time when you didn't understand what was happening.

How did you feel?

2. What happens to Jesus on the high mountain (verses 2-3)?

3. What two men talk to Jesus (verse 4)?

Note: Moses and Elijah were famous prophets who lived hundreds of years before Jesus.

4. What does the voice from the cloud say (verse 7)?

5. Look again at 8:29. How does this experience on the mountain show that Peter's words are right?

6. When can Jesus' followers tell others what they have seen (verse 9)?

7. Jesus' followers still have questions (verses 10, 11). How do you think they feel as they come down the mountain?

Note: The Jews expected Elijah to come back to prepare for the Messiah. Jesus said John the Baptist did Elijah's work (Matthew 17:11-13).

Read Mark 9:14-29

8. Sometimes our problems seem too big for any answer. What difficult problem do you or your friends have now?

9. While Jesus is on the mountain with Peter, James, and John, what is happening to his other followers (verse 14)?

10. What problem does the father have (verses 17-18)?

Read verses 19 and 23. What does Jesus say is the real problem of the people?

11. Why do you think Jesus talks to the father about what is wrong with the boy (verses 21, 22)?

12. How does the father answer Jesus' challenge about faith (verse 24)?

13. What is Jesus able to do even though the father has weak faith (verses 25-27)?

 14. How does this encourage you with difficult problems you have?

15. Why do you think Jesus' followers could not help the boy (verses 16, 18, 28, 29)?

Read Mark 9:30-41

 16. Why do people want to be great and powerful?

17. What big thing is Jesus thinking about as he and his followers walk through Galilee (verse 31)?

18. What are Jesus' followers thinking about as they travel along the road (verse 34)?

19. What does Jesus want his followers to understand about true greatness (verse 35)?

20. What does it mean to do something or accept someone in Jesus' name (verses 37, 41)?

Read Mark 9:42-50

21. Jesus gives four strong examples to show what is most important in life. What are they (verses 42-47)?

22. If sin is so serious, what can you do to control your hands, feet, and eyes?

23. What does Jesus say about salt (verse 50)?

24. How can we be like salt in the world?

Summary

1. In this chapter, what do you learn about Jesus?

2. In this chapter, what important things does Jesus teach his followers?

Prayer

Dear Jesus,
Thank you for showing me what is most important in life.
Help me to live for you. Help me to be like a child
trusting you, and not to think about my own greatness.
Help me to serve you always. Amen.

Mark 10

Jesus Teaches About Divorce

10 [1] Jesus went away from the city of Capernaum. He came to the country of Judea and to the other side of the Jordan River. Again the people gathered around Him. He began to teach them as He had been doing.
[2] The proud religious law-keepers came to Him. They tried to trap Him and asked, "Does the Law say a man can divorce his wife?" [3] He said to them, "What did the Law of Moses say?" [4] They said, "Moses allowed a man to divorce his wife, if he put it in writing and gave it to her." [5] Jesus said to them, "Because of your hard hearts, Moses gave you this Law. [6] From the beginning of the world, God made them man and woman. [7] Because of this, a man is to leave his father and mother and is to live with his wife. [8] The two will become one. So they are no longer two, but one. [9] Let no man divide what God has put together."
[10] In the house the followers asked Jesus about this again. [11] He said to them, "Whoever divorces his wife and marries another is not faithful to her and is guilty of a sex sin. [12] If a woman divorces her husband and marries another, she is not faithful to her husband and is guilty of a sex sin."

Jesus Gives Thanks For Little Children

[13] They brought little children to Jesus that He might put His hand on them. The followers spoke sharp words to those who brought them. [14] Jesus saw this and was angry with the followers. He said, "Let the little children come to Me. Do not stop them. The holy nation of God is made up of ones like these. [15] For sure, I tell you, whoever does not receive the holy nation of God as a little child does not go into it." [16] He took the children in His arms. He put His hands on them and prayed that good would come to them.

Jesus Teaches About Keeping the Law

[17] Jesus was going on His way. A man ran to Him and got down on his knees. He said, "Good Teacher, what must I do to have life that lasts forever?" [18] Jesus said to him, "Why do you call Me good? There is only One Who is good. That is God. [19] You know the Laws, 'Do not be guilty of sex sins in marriage. Do not kill another person. Do not take things from people in wrong ways. Do not steal. Do not lie. Respect your father and mother.' " [20] The man said to Jesus, "Teacher, I have obeyed all these Laws since I was a boy." [21] Jesus looked at him with love and said, "There is one thing for you to do yet. Go and sell everything you have and give the money to poor people. You will have riches in heaven. Then come and follow Me." [22] When the man heard these words, he was sad. He walked away with sorrow because he had many riches here on earth.

The Danger Of Riches

[23] Jesus looked around Him. He said to His followers, "How hard it is for rich people to get into the holy nation of God!" [24] The followers were surprised and wondered about His words. But Jesus said to them again, "Children! How hard it is for those who put their trust in riches to get into the holy nation of God! [25] It is easier for a camel to go through the eye of a needle than for a rich man to go to heaven."

[26] They were very surprised and wondered, saying to themselves, "Then who can be saved from this punishment of sin?" [27] Jesus looked at them and said, "This cannot be done by men but God can do anything."

[28] Then Peter began to say to Him, "We have given up everything we had and have followed You." [29] Jesus said, "For sure, I tell you, there are those who have given up houses or brothers or sisters or father or mother or wife or children or lands because of Me, and the Good News. [30] They will get back one hundred times as much now at this time in houses and in brothers and sisters and mothers and children and lands. Along with this, they will have very much trouble. And they will have life that lasts forever in the world to come. [31] Many who are first will be last. Many who are last will be first."

Jesus Tells Of His Death The Third Time

[32] They were on their way to Jerusalem. Jesus walked in front of them. Those who followed were surprised and afraid. Then Jesus took the twelve followers by themselves. He told them what would happen to Him. [33] He said, "Listen, we are going to Jerusalem. The Son of Man will be handed over to the religious leaders of the Jews and to the teachers of the Law. They will say that He must be put to death. They will hand Him over to the people who are not Jews. [34] They will make fun of Him and will beat Him. They will spit on Him and will kill Him. But three days later He will be raised from the dead."

James And John Ask Jesus Something Hard

[35] James and John, the sons of Zebedee, came to Jesus. They said, "Teacher, we would like to have You do for us whatever we ask You." [36] He said to them, "What would you like to have Me do for you?" They said to Him, "Let one of us sit by Your right side and the other by Your left side when You receive Your great honor in heaven." [38]Jesus said to them, "You do not know what you ask. Can you take the suffering I am about to take? Can you be baptized with the baptism that I am baptized with?" [39]They said to Him, "Yes, we can." Jesus said to them, "You will, for sure, suffer the way I will suffer. You will be baptized with the baptism that I am baptized with. [40] But to sit on My right side or on My left side is not for Me to give. It will be given to those for whom it has been made ready." [41] The other ten followers heard it. They were angry with James and John. [42] Jesus called them to Him and said, "You know that those who are made leaders over the nations show their power to the people. Important leaders use their power over the people. [43] It must not be that way with you. Whoever wants to be great among you, let him care for you. [44] Whoever wants to be first among you, must be the one who is owned and cares for all. [45] For the Son of Man did not come to be cared for. He came to care for others. He came to give His life so that many could be bought by His blood and be made free from sin."

Healing Of The Blind Man

[46] Then they came to the city of Jericho. When He was leaving the city with His followers and many people, a blind man was sitting by the road. He was asking people for food or money as they passed by. His name was Bartimaeus, the son of Timaeus. [47] He heard that Jesus of Nazareth was passing by. He began to speak with a loud voice, saying, "Jesus, Son of David, take pity on me!" [48] Many people spoke sharp words to the blind man telling him not to call out like that. But he spoke all the more. He said, "Son of David, take pity on me." [49] Jesus stopped and told them to call the blind man. They called to him and said, "Take hope! Stand up, He is calling for you!" [50] As he jumped up, he threw off his coat and came to Jesus. [51] Jesus said to him, "What do you want Me to do for you?" The blind man said to Him, "Lord, I want to see!" [52] Jesus said, "Go! Your faith has healed you." At once he could see and he followed Jesus down the road.

Asking the Right Questions

Mark 10

J esus continues his journey to Jerusalem. On the way, different people ask Jesus questions. Only two ask in the right way and receive what they want. Study this chapter carefully to see what Jesus wants to do for you.

Read Mark 10:1-12

1. What do you think makes a good marriage?

2. Why do the law-keepers question Jesus (verse 2)?

3. How does Jesus answer them (verse 3)?

Note: Moses' laws about divorce were not to make divorce easy, but more difficult.

4. What is God's plan about marriage (verses 6-9)?

5. Why is being faithful so important in a marriage?

Read Mark 10:13-16

6.   What does Jesus teach his followers about children by what he says and how he treats them (verses 14, 16)?

7.   How can you help children come to Jesus?

8.   How can you be more like a child in the way you come to Jesus?

Read Mark 10:17-31

9.   How would you feel if someone asked you to give away everything you have?

10. What do verses 17-22 tell you about the man who comes to Jesus?

11. What is this man looking for (verse 17)?

12. What keeps him from following Jesus (verse 22)?

13. The people thought that being rich was a sign of God's great blessing. What does Jesus say that surprises his followers (verse 23)?

14. Jesus says it is not possible to be saved by riches. How is salvation possible (verse 27)?

15. Peter says, "We have given up everything we had and have followed you" (verse 28). What does Jesus promise his followers (verses 29-31)?

16. Can you give some examples of how the promises Jesus made are true in the lives of people today?

Read Mark 10:32-34

17. Compare this paragraph with 8:31 and 9:31. What new things does Jesus tell about his future?

Read Mark 10:35-45

18. What do James and John want Jesus to do for them (verse 37)?

19. How does Jesus answer them (verses 38-40)?

20. What does Jesus teach about being a great and important person (verses 42-44)?

21. Verse 45 is one of the most important verses in Mark. What is the main purpose for Jesus' coming to earth?

Read Mark 10:46-52

22. What does the blind man ask Jesus in verses 47 and 48?

23. Why do you think Jesus asks him what he wants (verse 48)?

24. Why is this blind man healed (verse 52)?

Summary

1. Look again at all the questions or requests people asked Jesus in this chapter. Which ones received what they asked for?

2. If Jesus asked you, "What do you want me to do for you?" what would you say?

    What would be your part and what would be God's part?

Prayer

Dear Jesus,
Thank you that you came to give your life for me. Thank you that your death can make me free from sin. Give me faith and help me to trust you for every need I have. In your name I pray. Amen.

Mark 11

The Last Time Jesus Goes To Jerusalem

11 [1] Jesus and His followers were near Jerusalem at the Mount of Olives. They were in the towns of Bethphage and Bethany. Jesus sent two of His followers on ahead. [2] He said to them, "Go into the town over there. As soon as you get there, you will find a young donkey tied. No man has ever sat on it. Let the donkey loose and bring it here. [3] If anyone asks you, 'Why are you doing that?' say, 'The Lord needs it. He will send it back again soon.' "

[4] The two followers went on their way. They found the young donkey tied by the door where two streets crossed. They took the rope off its neck. [5] Some men were standing there. They said to the two followers, "Why are you taking the rope off that young donkey?" [6] The two followers told them what Jesus had said and the men let them take the donkey. [7] They brought it to Jesus and put their coats over it. Jesus sat on the donkey. [8] Many people put their clothes down on the road. Others cut branches off the trees and put them down on the road. [9] Those who went in front and those who followed spoke with loud voices, "Greatest One! Great and honored is He Who comes in the name of the Lord! [10] Great is the coming holy nation of our father David. It will come in the name of the Lord, Greatest One in the highest heaven."

[11] Jesus came to Jerusalem and went into the house of God. He looked around at everything. Then He went with the twelve followers to the town of Bethany because it was late.

The Fig Tree With No Fruit

¹² They came from Bethany the next morning. Jesus was hungry. ¹³ Along the road He saw a fig tree with leaves on it. He went over to see if it had any fruit. He saw nothing but leaves. It was not the right time for figs. ¹⁴ Jesus said to the tree, "Let no one ever again eat fruit from you." His followers heard Him say it.

Jesus Stops The Buying And
The Selling In The House Of God

¹⁵ Then they came to Jerusalem. Jesus went into the house of God. He began to make the people leave who were selling and buying in the house of God. He turned over the tables of the men who changed money. He turned over the seats of those who sold doves. ¹⁶ He would not allow anyone to carry a pot or pan through the house of God. ¹⁷ He taught them saying, "Is it not written, 'My house is to be called a house of prayer for all the nations'? You have made it a place of robbers."

¹⁸ The teachers of the Law and the religious leaders of the Jews heard it. They tried to find some way to put Jesus to death. But they were afraid of Him because all the people were surprised and wondered about His teaching. ¹⁹ When evening came Jesus and His followers went out of the city.

The Fig Tree Dries Up

²⁰ In the morning they passed by the fig tree. They saw it was dried up from the roots. ²¹ Peter remembered what had happened the day before and said to Jesus, "Teacher, see! The fig tree which You spoke to has dried up!" ²² Jesus said to them, "Have faith in God. ²³ For sure, I tell you, a person may say to this mountain, 'Move from here into the sea.' And if he does not doubt, but believes that what he says will be done, it will happen. ²⁴ Because of this, I say to you, whatever you ask for when you pray, have faith that you will receive it. Then you will get it. ²⁵ When you stand to pray, if you have anything against anyone, forgive him. Then your Father in heaven will forgive your sins also. ²⁶ *If you do not

forgive them their sins, your Father in heaven will not forgive your sins."

27 They came again to Jerusalem. Jesus was walking around in the house of God. The religious leaders and the teachers of the Law and other leaders came to Him. 28 They asked, "How do You have the right and the power to do these things? Who gave You the right and the power to do them?" 29 Jesus said to them, "I will ask you one thing also. If you tell Me, then I will tell you by what right and power I do these things. 30 Was the baptism of John from heaven or from men? Tell Me." 31 They talked among themselves. They said, "If we say from heaven, He will say, 'Why did you not believe him?' 32 But how can we say, 'From men'?" They were afraid of the people because everyone believed that John was one who spoke for God. 33 So they said, "We do not know." Then Jesus said, "Then I will not tell you by what right and power I do these things."

Jesus' Last Week

Mark 11

This chapter tells us about what happens on Sunday, Monday, and Tuesday of Holy Week. This is the last week of Jesus' life on earth. The leaders of the Jews plan how to kill Jesus.

Read Mark 11:1-11

 1. How does an important person usually come into a city?

2. As they come near Jerusalem, what does Jesus tell two of his followers to do (verse 2)?

3. Jesus sits on a young donkey to show the people that he is a royal person who comes in peace. What do the people do when Jesus comes into Jerusalem (verses 8-9)?

4. The people want Jesus to free them from the Roman government. Jesus doesn't think the same way. What is the first thing Jesus does when he comes into the city (verse 11)?

Why do you think he does this?

5. What would you think if Jesus came to the place where you live?

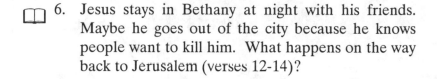

Read Mark 11:12-26

6. Jesus stays in Bethany at night with his friends. Maybe he goes out of the city because he knows people want to kill him. What happens on the way back to Jerusalem (verses 12-14)?

Note: This is a difficult story to understand. Some people who study the Bible think Jesus shows that Jerusalem looks like a beautiful city, but it doesn't have true faith. The fig tree looks like it may have fruit, but there isn't any. Both Israel and the fig tree look like they have something good, but they don't.

7. What happens in the temple (verses 15-17)?

8. Why does Jesus do this (verse 17)?

9. What do the religious leaders do, and why, when they see Jesus use his power in the Temple (verse 18)?

10. The next morning, how does the fig tree show that it is the same on the outside as the inside (verse 20)?

11. Do you give good things to Jesus in your life, or are you just like the fig tree that looks good but isn't?

12. What is something in your life that seems too big for God to be able to change?

What does Jesus teach his followers about prayer (verses 22-26)?

13. Why is it important that we look at the power of God and not how big our problems are?

14. What do we need so we can have answers to prayer (verses 22, 24, and 25)?

Read Mark 11:27-33

15. Who are people in your life that have power?

Where do they get it from?

16. What do the religious leaders ask Jesus about (verses 27, 28)?

17. Why do they ask these questions (verse 18)?

18. Why can't they answer Jesus' question about John (verses 31-33)?

19. The quote below is from the beginning of Mark:

"He preached, saying, 'One is coming after me Who is greater than I. I am not good enough to get down and help Him take off His shoes. I have baptized you with water. But He will baptize you with the Holy Spirit (Mark 1:7, 8).' "

What did John say about Jesus?

20. What did John's baptism show (1:4)?

Summary

1. What does Jesus show about himself by the way he acts in Jerusalem?

2. Why do people have different responses about who Jesus says he is?

Prayer

Dear Jesus,
Thank you for teaching us very important things about life. You teach us about who you are, how important your house of prayer is, and what we need to do when we pray. Thank you for showing us what is true by what you say and do. Amen.

Mark 12

The Picture-story Of The Grape-field

12 [1] Jesus began to teach them by using picture-stories, saying, "There was a man who planted grapes in a field. He put a fence around it and made a place for making wine. He built a tower to look over the field. Then he let farmers rent it and went into another country.

2 "The time came for gathering the grapes. He sent his servant to the farmers to get some of the grapes. [3] The farmers took him and beat him. They sent him back with nothing. [4] The owner sent another servant. The farmers threw stones at him and hit him on the head and did other bad things to him. [5] Again the owner sent another servant. The farmers killed that one. Many other servants were sent. They beat some and they killed others.

[6] "He had a much-loved son to send yet. So last of all he sent him to them, saying, 'They will respect my son.' [7] The farmers said to themselves, 'This is the one who will get everything when the owner dies. Let us kill him and we will get everything.' [8] They took him and killed him. They threw his body outside the field. [9] What will the owner of the field do? He will come and kill the farmers. He will give the field to other farmers.

[10] "Have you not read what the Holy Writings say? 'The Stone that was put aside by the workmen has become the most important Stone in the corner of the building. [11] The Lord has done this. It is great in our eyes.' " (Psalm 118:22-23) [12] The leaders wanted to take Him but they were afraid of the people. They knew He had told the picture-story against them. They left Him and went away.

They Try To Trap Jesus

[13] Some of the proud religious law-keepers and Herod's men were sent to trap Jesus in His talk. [14] They came to Him and said, "Teacher, we know You are true. We know You are not afraid of what men think or say about You. You teach the way of God in truth. Is it right to pay taxes to Caesar or not? [15] Should we pay or not pay?" Jesus knew how they pretended to be someone they were not. He said to them, "Why do you try to trap Me? Bring Me a small piece of money so I may look at it?" [16] They brought Him one. He asked them, "Whose picture is this? Whose name is on it?" They answered, "Caesar's." [17] Then Jesus said to them, "Pay to Caesar the things that belong to Caesar. Pay to God the things that belong to God." They were surprised and wondered at Him.

They Ask About Being Raised From The Dead

[18] Some people from the religious group who believe no one will be raised from the dead came to Jesus. They asked Him, [19] "Teacher, Moses gave us a Law. It said, 'If a man's brother dies and leaves his wife behind, but no children, then his brother should marry his wife and raise children for his brother.' (Deuteronomy 25:5) [20] There were seven brothers. The first was married. He died before he had any children. [21] The second married her and died. He had no children. The same happened with the third. [22] All seven had her for a wife. All died without children. Last of all the woman died. [23] When people are raised from the dead, whose wife will she be? All seven had her for a wife." [24] Jesus said to them, "Is this not the reason you are wrong, because you do not know the Holy Writings or the power of God? [25] When people are raised from the dead, they do not marry and are not given in marriage. They are like angels in heaven. [26] As for the dead being raised, have you not read in the book of Moses how God spoke to him in the burning bush? He said, 'I am the God of Abraham and the God of Isaac and God of Jacob.' (Exodus 3:2-6) [27] He is not the God of the dead, He is the God of the living. So you are very much wrong."

The Great Law

²⁸ Then one of the teachers of the Law heard them arguing. He thought Jesus had spoken well. He asked Him, "Which Law is the greatest of all?" ²⁹ Jesus said to him, "The greatest Law is this, 'Listen, Jewish people, The Lord our God is one Lord! ³⁰ You must love the Lord your God with all your heart and with all your soul and with all your mind and with all your strength.' (Deuteronomy 6:4-5) This is the first Law.

³¹ "The second Law is this: 'You must love your neighbor as yourself.' (Leviticus 19:18) No other Law is greater than these."

³² Then the teacher of the Law said, "Teacher, You have told the truth. There is one God. There is no other God but Him. ³³ A man should love Him with all his heart and with all his understanding. He should love Him with all his soul and with all his strength and love his neighbor as himself. This is more important than to bring animals to be burned on the altar or to give God other gifts on the altar in worship." ³⁴ Jesus saw he had spoken with understanding. He said to him, "You are not far from the holy nation of God." After that no one thought they could ask Him anything.

Jesus Asks The Proud Religious Law-keepers About The Christ

³⁵ Jesus was in the house of God teaching. He asked, "How do the teachers of the Law say that Christ is the Son of David? ³⁶ For David himself, led by the Holy Spirit, said, 'The Lord said to my Lord, sit at my right side until I make those who hate You a place to rest Your feet' (Psalm 110:1). ³⁷ David himself calls Him Lord. Then how can He be his son?" Many people were glad to hear Him.

False Teachers

³⁸ Jesus taught them, saying, "Look out for the teachers of the Law. They like to walk around in long coats. They like to have the respect of men as they stand in the center of town where people gather. ³⁹ They like to have the impor-

tant seats in the places of worship and the important places at big suppers. [40] They take houses from poor women whose husbands have died. They cover up the bad they do by saying long prayers. They will be punished all the more."

The Woman Whose Husband Had Died
Gave All She Had

[41] Jesus sat near the money box in the house of God. He watched the people putting in money. Many of them were rich and gave much money. [42] A poor woman whose husband had died came by and gave two very small pieces of money.

[43] Jesus called His followers to Him. He said, "For sure, I tell you, this poor woman whose husband has died has given more money than all the others. [44] They all gave of that which was more than they needed for their own living. She is poor and yet she gave all she had, even what she needed for her own living."

Teaching in the House of God

Mark 12

The Jewish leaders want to trap Jesus by their questions. They want to show the people that he should be killed. Jesus knows the reasons why people ask questions. Study this chapter to see how he answers difficult questions.

Read Mark 12:1-12

1. In this picture-story how do the farmers treat the servants and the son?

2. How is the owner's son described (verse 6)?

Note: In this story the owner is God, the vineyard is Israel. The farmers are the religious leaders. The servants are the early preachers. The son is Jesus.

3. What is Jesus saying about the future in this picture story?

4. In verses 10 and 11, Jesus tells another picture-story that has the same idea as the first. Who are the

workmen and who is the stone that the workmen put aside?

5. Jesus tells these stories to answer the leaders' question about his power (11:28). Now that he has answered them, how do the religious leaders feel about Jesus?

Read Mark 12:13-17

6. Why do the proud religious law-keepers and Herod's men come to Jesus (verse 13)?

7. How would this question trap Jesus if he answered yes or no?

8. What does Jesus know about the Jewish leaders (verse 15)?

9. How does Jesus answer their question?

10. What do you need to give to the government?

What do you need to give to God?

Read Mark 12:18-27

11. Another group of Jewish leaders who believe no one will be raised from the dead come to Jesus. What do they ask Jesus and why?

12. Jesus says they are wrong for several reasons. What are they (verses 24-28)?

13. What people in the Bible does Jesus talk about to show that he is right (verse 26)?

Read Mark 12:28-34

14. Why does the teacher of the law ask the question in verse 28?

15. The ten commandments God gave his people are told in Exodus 20:3-17. The first four tell how a person should act toward God. The last six tell how a person should act toward other people. How does Jesus include all ten commandments in his two statements (verses 29-31)?

 16. What do you think it means to love God and to love your neighbor as Jesus teaches?

Read Mark 12:35-37

17. What question does Jesus ask (verse 35)?

Note: The Jews in Jesus' time remembered David as their greatest king. While he was king the nation of Israel was free. They want Jesus as the Son of David to lead the people in the same way.

18. The teachers of the Law talk about the Christ as a man in the line of King David. How does Jesus explain that the Christ is more than that (verses 36, 37)?

Read Mark 12:38-44

19. How do some people use religion to make them look better than others?

20. How does Jesus describe the teachers of the law (verses 38-40)?

21. Why do you think these teachers will be punished all the more?

22. How is the poor woman different from the other people who gave money (verses 41-44)?

 23. What can you learn about giving from this woman?

Summary

1. Who asks Jesus difficult questions in this chapter?

2. Jesus uses the Bible to answer these questions. What important things does he teach?

3. What questions do people ask about Jesus today?

   Where should we find the answers?

Prayer

Dear Jesus,
Many people asked you difficult questions. You knew their hearts and answered their questions wisely. Help me to love God as you said to, with all my heart and mind and strength, and to love other people as I love myself. Amen.

Mark 13

Jesus Tells Of The House Of God

13 [1] Jesus went out of the house of God. One of His Followers said to Him, "Teacher, look at the big stones and these great buildings!" [2] Jesus said, "Do you see these great buildings? All these stones will be thrown down. Not one will be left standing on another."

Jesus Teaches On The Mount Of Olives

[3] Jesus sat down on the Mount of Olives at a place where He could see the house of God. Peter and James and John and Andrew came to Him. They asked without anyone else hearing, [4] "Tell us when this will be. What are we to look for when these things are to happen?"

What To Look For Before Jesus Returns

[5] Jesus began to say to them, "Be careful that no one leads you the wrong way [6] Many people will come using My name. They will say, 'I am Christ.' They will turn many to the wrong way. [7] When you hear of wars and much talk about wars, do not be surprised. These things have to happen. But the end is not yet. [8] Nations will have wars with other nations. Countries will fight against countries. The earth will shake and break apart in different places. There will be no food for people. There will be much trouble. These things are the beginning of much sorrow and pain.

It Will Be Hard For Those Who Believe

[9] "Watch out for yourselves. They will take you to the courts. In the places of worship they will beat you. You will be taken in front of rulers and in front of kings because of Me.

You will be there to tell them about Me. [10] The Good News must first be preached to all the nations.

[11] "When you are put into their hands, do not be afraid of what you are to say or how you are to say it. Whatever is given to you to say at that time, say it. It will not be you who speaks, but the Holy Spirit. [12] A brother will hand over a brother to death. A father will hand over his son. Children will turn against their parents and have them put to death. [13] You will be hated by all people because of Me. But he who stays true to the end will be saved.

Days Of Trouble And Pain And Sorrow

[14] "You will see a very sinful man-made god standing in the house of God where it has no right to stand. Then those in the country of Judea should run to the mountains. It was spoken of by the early preacher Daniel. (Daniel 9:27; 12:11) The one who reads this should understand. [15] He that is on the top of the house should not take the time to get anything out of his house. [16] He that is in the field should not go back to get his coat. [17] It will be hard for women who will soon be mothers. It will be hard for those feeding babies in those days! [18] Pray that it will not be during the winter. [19] In those days there will be much trouble and pain and sorrow. It has never been this bad from the beginning of time and never will be again. [20] If the Lord had not made those days short, no life would have been saved. Because of God's people whom He has chosen, He made the days short.

The False Religious Teachers

[21] "If anyone says to you, 'See! Here is the Christ,' or, 'There He is!' do not believe it. [22] Some will come who will say they are Christ. False preachers will come. These people will do special things for people to see. They will do surprising things, so that if it can be, God's people will be led to believe something wrong. [23] See! I have told you about these things before they happen.

Jesus Will Come Again In His Greatness

[24] "After those days of much trouble and pain and sorrow are over, the sun will get dark. The moon will not give light.

[25] The stars will fall from the sky. The powers in the heavens will be shaken. [26] Then they will see the Son of Man coming in the clouds with great power and shining-greatness. [27] He will send His angels. They will gather together God's people from the four winds. They will come from one end of the earth to the other end of heaven.

The Picture-story Of The Fig Tree

[28] "Now learn something from the fig tree. When the branch begins to grow and puts out its leaves, you know summer is near. [29] In the same way, when you see all these things happen, you know the Son of Man is near. He is even at the door. [30] For sure, I tell you, the people of this day will not pass away before all these things have happened.

[31] "Heaven and earth will pass away, but My Words will not pass away. [32] But no one knows the day or the hour. No! Not even the angels in heaven know. The Son does not know. Only the Father knows.

[33] "Be careful! Watch and pray. You do not know when it will happen. [34] The coming of the Son of Man is as a man who went from his house to a far country. He gave each one of his servants some work to do. He told the one standing at the door to watch. [35] In the same way, you are to watch also! You do not know when the Owner of the house will be coming. It may be in the evening or in the night or when the sun comes up or in the morning. [36] He may come when you are not looking for Him and find you sleeping. [37] What I say to you, I say to all. Watch!"

Jesus Talks about the Future

Mark 13

J esus still has many important things to teach his followers. Though he will soon leave them, he promises that he will come back again. Jesus warns his followers to be ready.

Read Mark 13:1-8

1. Give examples of how people can be led in the wrong way today.

2. Why does one of Jesus' followers begin this conversation (verse 1)?

3. The house of God was one of the most beautiful buildings in the world during Jesus' time. Some of the stones were forty feet long, twelve feet high, and eighteen feet wide. The house of God was the place where all the Jews worshiped, and where the priest made sacrifices to God. It was the most important place for the Jews. What does Jesus say about the house of God (verse 2)?

4. What do these four followers want to know about the future (verses 3, 4)?

    Why?

5. In verses 5 and 6, what does Jesus say to be careful of?

6. What things does Jesus say will happen (verses 7, 8)?

Read Mark 13:9-13

7. What will happen to Jesus' followers?

8. What is the reason for this sorrow and pain (verses 9, 13)?

9. What will make their pain and sorrow very hard (verse 12)?

    What promises does Jesus give to people who believe in him (verses 10, 11, 13)?

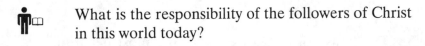 What is the responsibility of the followers of Christ in this world today?

Read Mark 13:14-23

10. Jesus' words remind the Jews of a time in history when sinful men put man-made gods in the house of God. Those were very bad days, and Jesus warns that this terrible thing will happen again in the house of God. What sign, warning, and advice does Jesus give (verses 14-16)?

11. Who will these days be very hard for (verse 17)?

12. Why will God make these days short (verse 20)?

Note: The believers in Jerusalem remembered what Jesus said. They quickly left the city of Jerusalem before the Romans destroyed it in A.D. 70.

13. What is another thing Jesus warns the people about (verses 21-23)?

 14. What do false preachers look like today?

Read Mark 13:24-37

15. What will happen when the Son of Man comes (verses 24-27)?

16. What else does Jesus teach about when these things in the future will happen (verses 28-29)?

17. What comfort does verse 31 give Jesus' followers?

18. What warning does Jesus give his followers in verse 32, 33?

19. What important idea does Jesus' story in verses 34-37 talk about?

Summary

1. Tell about the two things Jesus says will happen in the future.

2. What does Jesus tell you to do to stop people from leading you the wrong way?

Prayer

Dear Jesus,
You tell us what will happen when the end of this earth
comes. Sinful people will try to lead me the wrong way.
Help me to be careful, to watch, and to pray. Even
though this earth will pass away, your words will not.
Help me to obey what your words teach. Amen.

Mark 14:1-52

They Look For A Way To Put Jesus To Death

14 [1] It was now two days before the supper of the special religious gathering to remember how the Jews left Egypt and the supper of bread without yeast. The religious leaders and the teachers of the Law tried to trap Jesus. They tried to take Him so they could put Him to death. [2] These men said, "This must not happen on the day of the special supper. The people would be against it and make much trouble."

Mary Of Bethany Puts Special Perfume On Jesus

[3] Jesus was in the town of Bethany eating in the house of Simon. Simon was a man with a very bad skin disease. A woman came with a jar of special perfume. She had given much money for this. She broke the jar and poured the special perfume on the head of Jesus. [4] Some of them were angry. They said, "Why was this special perfume wasted? [5] This perfume could have been sold for much money and given to poor people." They spoke against her.

[6] Jesus said, "Let her alone. Why are you giving her trouble? She has done a good thing to Me. [7] You will have poor people with you all the time. Whenever you want, you can do something good for them. You will not have Me all the time. [8] She did what she could. She put this perfume on My body to make Me ready for the grave. [9] For sure, I tell you, wherever this Good News is preached in all the world, this woman will be remembered for what she has done."

Judas Hands Jesus Over To Be Killed

[10] Judas Iscariot was one of the twelve followers. He went to the head religious leaders of the Jews to talk about how he

might hand Jesus over to them. [11] When the leaders heard it, they were glad. They promised to give Judas money. Then he looked for a way to hand Jesus over.

Getting Ready For The Special Supper

[12] The first day of the supper of bread without yeast was the day to kill an animal. It was for the special religious gathering to remember how the Jews left Egypt. His followers said to Jesus, "What place do You want us to make ready for You to eat this special supper?" [13] Jesus sent two of His followers on ahead and said to them, "Go into the city. There a man carrying a jar of water will meet you. Follow him. [14] He will go into a house. You say to the owner of the house, "The Teacher asks, 'Where is the room you keep for friends, where I can eat this special supper with My followers?' " [15] He will take you to a large room on the second floor with everything in it. Make it ready for us."

[16] The followers went from there and came into the city. They found everything as Jesus had said. They made things ready for the special supper.

[17] In the evening He came with the twelve followers. [18]They sat at the table and ate. Jesus said, "For sure, I tell you, one of you will hand Me over to be killed. He is eating with Me." [19] They were very sad. They said to Him one after the other, "Is it I?" [20] He said to them, "It is one of the twelve followers. It is the one who is putting his hand with mine into the same dish. [21] The Son of Man is going away as it is written of Him. But it will be bad for that man who hands the Son of Man over to be killed! It would have been better if he had not been born!"

The First Lord's Supper

[22] As they were eating, Jesus took a loaf of bread. He gave thanks and broke it in pieces. He gave it to them and said, "Take, eat, this is My body." [23] Then He took the cup and gave thanks. He gave it to them and they all drank from it. [24] He said to them, "This is my blood of the New Way of Worship which is given for many. [25] For sure, I tell you, that I will not drink of the fruit of the vine until that day when I

drink it new in the holy nation of God." [26] After they sang a song, they went out to the Mount of Olives.

Jesus Tells How Peter Will Lie About Him

[27] Jesus said to them, "All of you will be ashamed of Me and leave Me tonight. For it is written, ' I will kill the shepherd and the sheep of the flock will spread everywhere.' (Zechariah 13:7) [28] After I am raised from the dead, I will go before you into the country of Galilee."

[29] Peter said to Him, "Even if all men are ashamed of You and leave You, I never will." [30] Jesus said to him, "For sure, I tell you, that today, even tonight, before a rooster crows two times, you will say three times you do not know Me." [31] Peter spoke with strong words, "Even if I have to die with You, I will never say that I do not know You." All the followers said the same thing.

Jesus Prays In Gethsemane

[32] They came to a place called Gethsemane. Jesus said to His followers, "You sit here while I pray." [33] He took Peter and James and John with Him. He began to have much sorrow and a heavy heart. [34] He said to them, "My soul is very sad. My soul is so full of sorrow I am ready to die. You stay here and watch." [35] He went a little farther and got down with His face on the ground. He prayed that this time of suffering might pass from Him if it could. [36] He said, "Father, You can do all things. Take away what must happen to Me. Even so, not what I want, but what You want."

[37] Then Jesus came to the followers and found them sleeping. He said to Peter, "Simon, are you sleeping? Were you not able to watch one hour? [38] Watch and pray so that you will not be tempted. Man's spirit wants to do this, but the body does not have the power to do it."

[39] Again Jesus went away and prayed saying the same words. [40] He came back and found them sleeping again. Their eyes were heavy. They did not know what to say to Him. [41] He came the third time and said to them, "Are you still sleeping and resting? It is enough! Listen, the time has come when the Son of Man will be handed over to sinners.

⁴² Get up and let us go. See! The man who will hand Me over to the head religious leader is near."

Jesus Handed Over To Sinners

⁴³ At once, while Jesus was talking, Judas came. He was one of the twelve followers. He came with many other men who had swords and sticks. They came from the head religious leaders of the Jews and the teachers of the Law and the leaders of the people. ⁴⁴ The man who was going to hand Jesus over gave the men something to look for. He said, "The Man I kiss is the One. Take hold of Him and take Him away."

⁴⁵ At once Judas went straight to Jesus and said, "Teacher!" and kissed Him. Then they put their hands on Him and took Him.

⁴⁷ One of the followers of Jesus who stood watching took his sword. He hit the servant owned by the head religious leader and cut off his ear. ⁴⁸ Jesus said to them, "Have you come with swords and sticks to take Me as if I were a robber? ⁴⁹ I have been with you every day teaching in the house of God. You never took hold of Me. But this has happened as the Holy Writings said it would happen." ⁵⁰ Then all His followers left Him and ran away.

⁵¹ A young man was following Him with only a piece of cloth around his body. They put their hands on the young man. ⁵² Leaving the cloth behind, he ran away with no clothes on.

The Last Supper: Judas Hands Jesus Over to Be Killed

Mark 14:1-52

T his is the last evening that the followers are with Jesus. They eat a special supper with him and then go to a garden to pray. Study this chapter and think about what you would see, hear, and feel if you could be a part of this story.

Read Mark 14:1-11

 1. What kind of gift do you give a special person who will soon leave?

2. Compare the different ways these people think about Jesus in verses 1-11:

    -the religious leaders

    -the woman

    -Judas

3. Some people are angry at the woman for wasting special perfume. How does Jesus answer them (verses 3-9)?

4. The woman does the best thing she can think of for Jesus. What good thing could you do for Jesus?

Read Mark 14:12-26

5. How does Jesus get ready for the special supper (verses 12-16)?

6. What does Jesus tell his followers while they eat (verse 18)?

7. What do the followers feel and think (verse 19)?

8. What does Jesus teach his followers in verses 22-25?

Note: Before the time of Jesus, the Jews put an animal to death on an altar in the house of God to show they were sorry for their sins. In the New Way of Worship Jesus gives his blood so that everyone's sins can be forgiven.

Read Mark 14:27-31

9. Sometimes people say they will do something. Then when it is time for them to do what they said, they can't. When have you seen this happen?

10. When Jesus says his followers will run away, what does Peter say he will do (verses 29, 31)?

    Why do you think Peter says this?

11. What does Jesus know about Peter that Peter does not yet know about himself (verse 30)?

12. Jesus knows when you are strong and when you are weak. How does that make you feel?

Why?

Read Mark 14:32-42

13. How do you help someone whose soul is so full of sorrow he is ready to die?

14. What does Jesus ask these three followers to do (verses 33, 34)?

15. What do you see in the heart and mind of Jesus (verses 33-36)?

16. Why do Jesus' followers go to sleep when Jesus asks them to watch and pray?

What does Jesus do and say to them?

Read Mark 14:43-52

17. If you could be in the garden with Jesus, what would you see, hear, and feel?

18. Who comes to take Jesus away (verse 43)?

19. What does Jesus do? What does he say (verses 48, 49)?

20. How have Jesus' words from verse 27 come true (verse 50)?

Summary

1. What do you learn about Jesus:

    in the town of Bethany (verses 1-11)?

    at the last supper (verses 12-25)?

    at the Mount of Olives (verses 27-52)?

2. What do you learn about Jesus' friends?

3. What do you learn about Jesus' enemies?

Prayer

Dear Jesus,
You went through so much pain and sorrow during your last days on earth. You know what it is like when I face difficult times in my life. Thank you for giving me an example of how to pray and face very hard things. Thank you for understanding me when I feel full of pain and sorrow in my life. Amen.

Mark 14:53–15:15

Jesus Stands In Front Of The Head Religious Leaders

14 [53] They led Jesus away to the head religious leader. All the religious leaders and other leaders and the teachers of the Law were gathered there. [54] But Peter followed a long way behind as they went to the house of the head religious leader. He sat with the helpers and got warm by the fire.

Jesus Stands In Front Of The Court

[55] The religious leaders and all the court were looking for something against Jesus. They wanted to find something so they could kill Him. But they could find nothing. [56] Many came and told false things about Him, but their words did not agree. [57] Some got up and said false things against Him. They said, [58] "We have heard Him say, 'I will destroy the house of God that was made with hands. In three days I will build another that is not made with hands.'" [59] Even these who spoke against Him were not able to agree.

[60] The head religious leader stood up in front of the people. He asked Jesus, "Have You nothing to say? What about the things these men are saying against You?" [61] Jesus said nothing. Again the head religious leader asked Him, "Are You the Christ, the Son of the Holy One?" [62] Jesus said, "I am! And you will see the Son of Man seated on the right side of the All-powerful God. You will see Him coming again in the clouds of the sky."

[63] Then the head religious leader tore his clothes apart. He said, "Do we need other people to speak against Him? [64] You have heard Him speak as if He were God! What do you think?" They all said He was guilty of death. [65] Some began to spit on Him. They covered Jesus' face, and they hit Him. They said, "Tell us what is going to happen." Soldiers hit Him with their hands.

Peter Said He Did Not Know Jesus

[66] Peter was outside in the yard. One of the servant-girls of the head religious leader came. [67] She saw Peter getting warm. She looked at him and said, "You were with Jesus of Nazareth." [68] Peter lied, saying, "I do not know Jesus and do not understand what you are talking about." As he went out, a rooster crowed.

[69] The servant-girl saw him again. She said to the people standing around, "This man is one of them." [70] He lied again saying that he did not know Jesus. Later, those who stood around said to Peter again, "For sure you are one of them. You are from the country of Galilee. You talk like they do." [71] He began to say strong words and to swear. He said, "I do not know the Man you are talking about!" [72] At once a rooster crowed the second time. Peter remembered what Jesus had said to him, "Before a rooster crows two times, you will say three times you do not know Me." When he thought about it, he cried.

Jesus Before Pilate

15 [1] Early in the morning the head religious leaders of the Jews and other leaders and the teachers of the Law and all the court gathered together to talk about Jesus. Then they tied up Jesus and led Him away. They handed Him over to Pilate. [2] Pilate asked Jesus, "Are You the King of the Jews?" He said to Pilate, "What you say is true."

[3] The religious leaders spoke many things against Him. Jesus did not say a word. [4] Pilate asked Him again, "Have You nothing to say? Listen to the things they are saying against You!" Jesus did not say a word. Pilate was much surprised and wondered about it.

Jesus Or Barabbas Is To Go Free

[6] Each year at the special supper Pilate would let one person who was in prison go free. It would be the one the people asked for. [7] The name of one of those in prison was Barabbas. He, together with others, had killed people while working against the leaders of the country. [8] All the people

went to Pilate and asked him to do as he had done before. [9] Pilate said, "Do you want me to let the King of the Jews go free?" [10] He knew the religious leaders had handed Jesus over to him because they were jealous. [11] The religious leaders talked the people into thinking that Pilate should let Barabbas go free. [12] Pilate said to them again, "What do you want me to do with the Man you call the King of the Jews?" [13] They spoke with loud voices again, "Nail Him to a cross." [14] Then Pilate said to them, "Why? What bad thing has He done?" They spoke with loud voices all the more, "Nail Him to a cross!"

The Crown Of Thorns

[15] Pilate wanted to please the people. He gave Barabbas to them and had Jesus beaten. Then He handed Him over to be nailed to a cross.

Jesus Stands in Front of the Court

Mark 14:53–15:15

A ll the religious leaders look for something against Jesus so they can kill him. They say false things about Jesus to show he is guilty. Study this chapter to see who Jesus says he is.

Read Mark 14:53-65

1. Where does the crowd take Jesus and who is there?

2. What problem does the court have when they want to say something against Jesus?

3. Why does Jesus choose to answer the head religious leader's question about his being the Christ, and not the things said against him?

4. The head religious leader tears his clothes when Jesus says he is the Christ, because he thinks that Jesus speaks like he is God (verses 62-64). What do the people in the court do to Jesus?

Read Mark 14:66-72

5. Tell about a time in your life when you were very disappointed in yourself.

6. What does verse 54 show about Peter?

7. Three times people in the courtyard talk to Peter. What do they say each time, and what does Peter answer?

8. What does verse 72 show us about Peter?

9. What are the different feelings Peter has in these verses?

10. How are you sometimes like Peter?

Read Mark 15:1-15

11. Give an example of leaders today who make decisions to make people happy instead of doing what is right.

12. The Jewish leaders take Jesus to Pilate. If Jesus is to be killed, the Roman courts have to condemn him. How are the questions of Pilate and the Jewish leader different (15:2; 14:61)?

13. How are Jesus' answers similar (14:62; 15:2, 4)?

14. What does Pilate do every year during the special supper (verse 6)?

15. What do you know about Barabbas?

16. Pilate knows the reason why the Jewish leaders hand Jesus over to him. What is it (verse 10)?

17. Read out loud Pilate's three questions in verses 9, 12, and 14. What do these questions show about Pilate?

18. What do the answers to these questions show us about the religious leaders and the crowd?

19. Why does Pilate make the decision he does?

 20. When do you want to do what others want instead of doing what is right?

Summary

1. What do you learn about Jesus when he stands in front of the religious leaders and Pilate?

2. Look at the two times Jesus is in court. How does Jesus show that he is on trial because he says he is Christ, the Son of the Holy One?

Prayer

Dear Jesus,
When you stood in front of the leaders, you were alone. The Jewish leaders and Pilate thought about themselves and did not care what was right. Help me to choose to do the right thing even if I need to stand alone. Amen.

Mark 15:16-47

The Crown Of Thorns

15 [16] The soldiers led Jesus away to a large room in the court. They called all the soldiers together. [17]The soldiers put a purple coat on Him. They put a crown of thorns on His head, [18] and said to Him, "Hello, King of the Jews!" [19] They hit Him on the head with a stick and spit on Him. They got down on their knees and worshiped Him. [20]After they had made fun of Him, they took the purple coat off of Him and put His own clothes back on Him. Then they led Him away to be nailed to a cross.

[21] They came to a man called Simon who was coming from the country of Cyrene. He was the father of Alexander and Rufus. They made Simon carry the cross of Jesus.

Jesus On The Cross

[22] They led Jesus to a place called Golgotha. This name means the place of the skull. [23] They gave Him wine with something in it to take away the pain, but He would not drink it. [24] When they had nailed Jesus to the cross, they divided His clothes by drawing names to see what each man should take. [25] It was about nine o'clock in the morning when they nailed Him to the cross. [26] Over Jesus' head they put in writing what they had against Him, the King of the Jews.

The Two Robbers

[27] They nailed two robbers on crosses beside Jesus. One was on His right side and the other was on His left side. [28] *It happened as the Holy Writings said it would happen, "They thought of Him as One Who broke the Law." (Isaiah 53:12)

[29] Those who walked by shook their heads and laughed at Jesus. They said, "You were the One Who could destroy the house of God and build it again in three days. [30] Save Yourself and come down from the cross." [31] The head religious leaders and the teachers of the Law made fun of Him also. They said to each other, "He saved others but He cannot save Himself. [32] Let Christ, the King of the Jews, come down from the cross. We want to see it and then we will believe." Those who were on the crosses beside Jesus spoke bad things to Him.

The Death Of Jesus

[33] From noon until three o'clock it was dark over all the land. [34] At three o'clock Jesus cried with a loud voice, "My God, My God, why have You left Me alone?"

[35] When some of those who stood by heard that, they said, "Listen! He is calling for Elijah." [36] One of them ran and took a sponge and filled it with sour wine. He put it on a stick and gave it to Him to drink. He said, "Let Him alone. Let us see if Elijah will come and take Him down."

The Powerful Works At The Time Of His Death

[37] Then Jesus gave a loud cry. He gave up His spirit and died. [38] The curtain in the house of God was torn in two from top to bottom. [39] The captain of the soldiers was looking at Jesus when He cried out. He saw Him die and said, "For sure, this Man was the Son of God."

The Women At The Cross

[40] Women were looking on from far away. Among them was Mary Magdalene and Mary the mother of the younger James and of Joses, and Salome. [41] These cared for Him when He was in the country of Galilee. There were many other women there who had followed Him to Jerusalem.

The Grave Of Jesus

[42] It was the day to get ready for the Day of Rest and it was now evening. [43] Joseph, who was from the city of Arimathea, was an important man in the court. He was looking for the

holy nation of God. Without being afraid, he went to Pilate and asked for the body of Jesus. [44] Pilate was surprised and wondered if Jesus was dead so soon. He called the captain of the soldiers and asked if Jesus was already dead.

[45] After the captain said that Jesus was dead, Pilate let Joseph take the body. [46] Joseph took the body of Jesus down from the cross. He put the linen cloth he had bought around the body. Then he laid the body in a grave which had been cut out in the side of a rock. He pushed a stone over to cover the door of the grave. [47] Mary Magdalene and Mary the mother of Joses saw where He was laid.

Jesus Is Nailed to a Cross and Put in a Grave

Mark 15:16-47

I n this study, Mark tells about the saddest day in history. It seems that Jesus' life is finished. But God uses the actions of sinful people for his own plan. He lets his own Son die so we can be saved from death.

Read Mark 15:16-32

1. What is it like to be with someone who is dying?

2. How do the words of Jesus in Mark 10:33-34 become true in verses 16-20?

3. What pain and sorrow do you think Jesus feels in his mind, body, and soul?

4. What do you know about Simon, and how do you think he feels (verse 21)?

5. What time of day is Jesus nailed to the cross?

6. There are verses in Psalms that talk about what will happen to Jesus:

Psalm 22:18–"They divide my clothes among them by drawing names to see who would get them."

Psalms 22:6-8–"But I am a worm and not a man. I am put to shame by men, and am hated by the people. All who see me make fun of me. They open their mouths and shake their heads, and say, 'He trusts in the Lord. Let the Lord help him. Let the Lord take him out of trouble, because he is happy in Him.' "

What is the same in Mark 15:24 and 29-32?

7. Read Mark 10:45 and 14:24. Why doesn't Jesus come down from the cross (15:30)?

8. How do the religious leaders show that they understand who Jesus says he is, but will not believe and follow him (verses 31, 32)?

Read Mark 15:33-41

9. Read verses 33, 34, 38, and 39. How is Jesus' death different from the death of other people?

10. Why does Jesus have to be separated from God?

11. What do some people think Jesus says (verse 35)?

12. What does the action of one of the people show us (verse 36)?

13. A heavy curtain hung in front of the holiest place in the house of God. The head religious leader went behind the curtain once a year to put a gift on the al-

tar for the sins of the people. What does the way the curtain is torn show us?

14. Why is the way now open for people to come to God?

15. What does the captain of the soldiers see (verse 39)?

16. Why do you think he says, "This man is really the Son of God?"

17. Who are the other people who see Jesus die (verses 40, 41)?

18. What do you think it was like to be with Jesus when he died?

19. Why did Jesus have to die (10:45)?

20. How are you a part of the reason for Jesus' death?

Read Mark 15:42-47

21. What happens when Joseph goes to see Pilate?

22. What do you learn about Joseph?

23. What does Joseph do with the body of Jesus?

24. It might be dangerous for Joseph to ask for the body of Jesus. Why does he do this?

25. In what areas of your life do you need to be like Joseph?

Summary

Ask each person in the group to choose one of the people in this chapter and tell about what happened during the day Jesus died. (Example: What did the captain of the soldiers or Simon of Cyrene or the women see and feel?)

Prayer

Dear Jesus,
Now we know we can go into the holiest place of all because you gave your blood. We now come to God by the new and living way you made for us. Help us to come near to God with a heart full of faith. Amen.

Note: The book of Mark ends at Mark 16:8. We will finish by using Luke, chapter 24, in our study of the life of Jesus Christ.

Mark 16:1-8; Luke 24

Jesus Is Raised From The Dead

16 ¹ The Day of Rest was over. Mary Magdalene and Mary the mother of James, and Salome bought spices. They wanted to put the spices on Jesus' body. ² Very early in the morning on the first day of the week, they came to the grave. The sun had come up. ³ They said to themselves, "Who will roll the stone away from the door of the grave for us?" ⁴ But when they looked, they saw the very large stone had been rolled away.

⁵ They went into the grave. There they saw a young man with a long white coat sitting on the right side. They were afraid. ⁶ He said, "Do not be afraid. You are looking for Jesus of Nazareth Who was nailed to a cross. He is risen! He is not here! See, here is the place where they laid Him. ⁷ Go and tell His followers and Peter that He is going ahead of you into Galilee. You will see Him there as He told you." ⁸ They ran from the grave shaking and were surprised. They did not say anything to anyone because they were afraid.

Jesus Is Raised From The Dead

Luke 24 ¹ Early in the morning on the first day of the week, the women went to the grave taking the spices they had made ready. ² They found the stone had been pushed away from the grave. ³ They went in but they did not find the body of the Lord Jesus.

⁴ While they wondered about what had happened, they saw two men standing by them in shining clothes. ⁵ They were very much afraid and got down with their faces to the ground. The men said to them, "Why do you look for the living One among those who are dead? ⁶ He is not here. He is risen. Do you not remember what He said to you when He was yet in Galilee? ⁷ He said, 'The Son of Man must be given over into the hands of sinful men. He must be nailed to a cross. He will rise again three days later.' " ⁸ They remembered what He had said.

⁹ When they come back from the grave, they told all these things to the eleven followers and to all the others. ¹⁰ They were Mary Magdalene and Joanna and Mary the mother of James. Other women who were with them told these things to the followers also. ¹¹ Their words sounded like foolish talk. The followers did not believe them. ¹² But Peter got up and ran to the grave. He got down to look in and saw only the linen clothes. Then he went away, surprised about what had happened.

The Followers Of Jesus Do Not Believe He Is Risen

¹³ That same day two of His followers were going to the town of Emmaus. It was about a two-hour walk from Jerusalem. ¹⁴ They talked of all these things that had happened. ¹⁵ While they were talking together, Jesus Himself came and walked along with them. ¹⁶ Something kept their eyes from seeing Who He was. ¹⁷ He said to them, "What are you talking about as you walk?" They stood still and looked sad. ¹⁸ One of them, whose name was Cleopas, said to Him, "Are you the only one visiting Jerusalem who has not heard of the things that have happened here these days?" ¹⁹ Jesus said to them, "What things?" They answered, "The things about Jesus of Nazareth. He was the great One Who spoke for God. He did Powerful works and spoke powerful words in the sight of God and the people. ²⁰ And the religious leaders and the leaders of the people gave Him over to be killed and nailed Him to a cross. ²¹ We were hoping He was the One Who was going to make the Jewish people free. But it was three days ago when these things happened.

²² "Some of the women of our group have surprised us and made us wonder. They went to the grave early this morning.

[23] They did not find His body. They came back saying they had seen angels in a special dream who said that He was alive. [24] Some of those who were with us went to the grave and found it as the women had said. But they did not see Him."

[25] Then Jesus said to them, "You foolish men. How slow you are to believe what the early preachers have said. [26] Did not Christ have to go through these hard things to come into His shining-greatness?" [27] Jesus kept on telling them what Moses and all the early preachers had said about Him in the Holy Writings.

[28] When they came to the town where they were going, Jesus acted as if He were going farther. [29] But they said to Him, "Stay with us. It will soon be evening. The day is about over." He went in to stay with them. [30] As He sat at the table with them, He took the bread and gave thanks and broke it. Then He gave it to them. [31] And their eyes were opened and they knew Him. Then He left them and could not be seen. [32] They said to each other, "Were not our hearts filled with joy when He talked to us on the road about what the Holy Writings said?"

[33] Then they got up at once and went back to Jerusalem. They found the eleven followers together and others with them. [34] They said, "For sure the Lord is risen and was seen by Simon." [35] Then they told what had happened on the road and how they came to know Him when He broke the bread.

Jesus Is Seen By The Other Ten Followers

[36] As they talked, Jesus Himself stood among them. He said, "May you have peace." [37] But they were afraid and full of fear. They thought they saw a spirit. [38] Jesus said to them, "Why are you afraid? Why do you have doubts in your hearts? [39] Look at My hands and My feet. See! It is I, Myself! Touch Me and see for yourself. A spirit does not have flesh and bones as I have." [40] When Jesus had said this, He showed them His hands and feet.

[41] They still wondered. It was hard for them to believe it and yet it made them happy. Then He said to them, "Do you have anything here to eat?" [42] They gave Jesus a piece

of fish that had been cooked and some honey. [43] He took it and ate it in front of them.

Jesus Sends His Followers To Teach

[44] Jesus said to them, "These are the things I told you while I was yet with you. All things written about Me in the Law of Moses and in the Books of the early preachers and in the Psalms must happen as they said they would happen." [45] Then He opened their minds to understand the Holy Writings. [46] He said to them, "It is written that Christ should suffer and be raised from the dead after three days. [47] It must be preached that men must be sorry for their sins and turn from them. Then they will be forgiven. This must be preached in His name to all nations beginning in Jerusalem. [48] You are to tell what you have seen. [49] See! I will send you what My Father promised. But you are to stay in Jerusalem until you have received power from above."

Jesus Goes To Be Beside His Father

[50] Jesus led them out as far as Bethany. Then He lifted up His hands and prayed that good would come to them. [51] And while He was praying that good would come to them, He went from them (*and was taken up to heaven and [52] they worshiped Him). Then they went back to Jerusalem with great joy. [53] They spent all their time in the house of God honoring and giving thanks to God.

Jesus Comes Back to Life

Mark 16:1-8; Luke 24

C hapter 15 tells about how Jesus was nailed to a cross and killed. The earliest copies of the book of Mark end at Mark 16:8. However, Jesus' life is not finished yet. The story is not over! For a clear explanation of Jesus being raised from the dead, we will study Luke 24 with Mark 16:1-8. Study these chapters carefully to understand the greatest power Jesus has.

Read Mark 16:1-8

1. What do you think the women say and feel as they go to the grave?

   What do they see and learn at the grave?

2. Look at Jesus' words in 14:28. Why should the women not be afraid?

3. What do the women do after the angel talks to them?

Read Luke 24:1-12

4. What does Luke add in 24:1-12 to Mark's story about the women?

5. Why don't the followers believe what the women tell them (verse 11)?

Read Luke 24:13-35

6. What do the two followers on the way to Emmaus think and talk about?

   Why are they so sad?

7. What questions does Jesus ask these two followers?

8. Why does Jesus talk about what Moses and all the early preachers say about him in the Holy Writings before showing them who he is?

9. Why do these sad followers ask Jesus to stay with them?

10. When do these two see that the man at their table is Jesus?

11. Why do they walk the seven miles back to Jerusalem?

    What do they learn when they get there?

12. If you had to explain how Jesus lived, died, and was raised to life, what would you say?

Read Luke 24:36-43

13. Why are the followers afraid when they see Jesus?

14. What does Jesus say about himself (verse 39)?

15. Why does Jesus ask them for something to eat?

Read Luke 24:44-49

16. What does Jesus want his followers to understand about the Law of Moses, the Books of the early preachers, and the Psalms (verses 44-46)?

17. What special help does Jesus give them (verse 45)?

18. Why is it important for Jesus' followers then and now to understand the Holy Writings?

19. What information does Jesus give about what must be preached (verses 46-48)?

20. Why will Jesus' followers need power from heaven?

Read Luke 24:50-53

21. How does Jesus leave his followers (verses 50, 51)?

22. What do his followers do when Jesus leaves?

Summary

1. What do you learn about the kind of body Jesus has after he is raised from the dead?

   Look at Luke 24:3-6, 12, 15, 17, 30, 34, and 36-43.

2. How does Jesus' return from death change his followers?

3. What difference does Jesus' return from death make to you today?

Prayer

Dear Jesus,
You were raised from the dead and this completed your work here on earth to save all people. This shows that you win over sin and death. It shows that you are the Son of God. Thank you for showing me who you are. Help me to follow you always. Amen.

Who is Jesus? The book of Mark teaches that Jesus is the Son of God. The story shows Jesus' power as he teaches and does many miracles. This book also tells about the death of Jesus for the sins of everyone. Jesus did not stay in the grave! He is alive today and has the same power. Jesus teaches that we must believe in him and turn away from our sins. If we do this, we will live forever with him.

What will you decide about Jesus Christ? If you want to follow Jesus, you may pray:

Dear Jesus,
Thank you for showing me your power through your teaching and your miracles. Thank you for showing your love for me by dying on the cross. I believe you are the Son of God. Forgive my sins. I choose to love you with all my heart, soul, mind, and strength. Help me to obey your teaching and follow you always. Amen.